DOWNLINE
WHISPERING

The Art of Knowing and
Growing Your Team

BETH WHICKER

Editors:
Jake Whicker, Mindi Jacob and Andy Jacob

Cover Design:
Kasia Gilbert

ISBN-10: 1974192911
ISBN-13: 978-1974192915

ADVANCE PRAISE

"Not just another theory, Downline Whispering is practical, step by step directions in how you can know your downline, pinpoint areas of growth and those that need attention, all while building and training leaders in your team to do the same. Downline Whispering is a must for any leader looking to stir up momentum, work smarter not harder, and create connection. Beth lays it out so simply, and I only wish I had started this on day one. I have taken my team through this training twice now, and each time, I'm blown away by the growth in my downline, the connections made, and the leaders that emerge. Do yourself a solid and get your entire team a copy."
Mary Leigh Brown, Gold Leader, Tennessee

"Downline Whispering is a system that I wish God had led me to long before now. I have been a part of other direct sales companies, and there was always something missing. I am huge into connection, relationships and making sure that my team knows that I am (almost) always available for them. Downline Whispering gives a practical guide to making sure that my goals as a team leader are always accomplished. I have worked years trying to pinpoint the exact steps to keep in contact with my team and how to help make sure things don't just slip through the cracks. I now have a system that allows me to keep tabs on my team growth and encourage, educate and elevate those on my team based on the season they are in. Communication is the key to any relationship, including business. Downline Whispering is where it's at! Save yourself from wasting a lot of time spinning wheels and getting nowhere and grab Downline Whispering now!"
Melissa Patton, Executive Leader, Florida

"Downline Whispering helped me stay in the know for each person I helped get started on their journey with essential oils by keeping me organized. I am a "creative personality type" who has trouble with follow up. Watching out for my downline using these steps grew my business from a neat hobby to a full-blown business with lives changed and people truly educated on how to better care for themselves and their families."
Devyn Rae Winchell - Silver Leader, California

"Downline Whispering is paramount to success in this business. Personal attention is the top priority for our team, and Downline Whispering allows us to maintain relationships and care for those connected to us. Something as small as a friendly reminder of an upcoming order doesn't go unnoticed. Thanks to Beth's leadership while implementing and teaching this practice to her team, we have seen unbelievable growth."
Crystal Jackson, Executive Leader, Florida

"Downline Whispering is a vital and necessary part of growing your Young Living business. Incorporating these practices over the course of time will set your team apart. Beth has not only mastered the art of Downline Whispering in her own business to maximize her team's growth, but she's now selflessly sharing her method with us in an easily replicable process that we can all learn to help us to be successful."
Shelby Paulk, Diamond, Michigan

"Downline Whispering is a breath of fresh air in the journey of being a leader. Beth shows you how to lead by loving on and knowing your team. Downline Whispering is a work of heart that will help you discover the basics of what you need to be doing, why you should be doing it, and how to do the best you can. This is a game changer."
Mary Clendenin, Platinum, North Carolina

DEDICATION

To Jake, You are a big reason this book is what it is. You have not only helped me weave my story throughout, but have inspired me in so many ways. You are a gentle, strong, godly man. You are my best friend and the love of my life. You have helped me to see that I am beautiful and loved and chosen. Thank you, Jake. For everything.

To Katelynn, Halee, Karis & Jett, Thank you for making me the woman and the mother I am today. Thank you for allowing me to make mistakes and loving me through them. I love each one of you fiercely. The four of you have my heart. Forever.

To my team, You are why I'm here today. I could not and would not be able to do this without you. You inspire me. You amaze me. Thank you for trusting me to lead you despite my flaws and ridiculous ideas that sometimes don't work out. Thank you for forgiving me when I say stupid things. Thank you for believing in our team. To Diamond and beyond, my friends. I believe in each one of you.

To Mindi, Kasia, Amy & Jess, Thank goodness you guys put up with my crazy. Whenever I throw you guys an idea, you are there to catch it and help me run with it. I appreciate your friendship more than you know.

To my crossline friends. Thank you for your constant love and encouragement. I'm thankful that we can cheer each other on without jealousy or competition. Let's continue to change the world. Together.

BETH WHICKER

CONTENTS

Foreword

On November 30, 2013, a new member, Beth Whicker, showed up in my downline. Little did I know that she would not only change the entire face of my Young Living team, but she would also become a dear friend. I have watched as Beth has grown an AMAZING organization by loving on her people. She loves hard. That love has transitioned into a business model that not only has built an impressive structure that any person would be proud of, but has brought her closer to those who are part of that organization. She pours into them, she knows their stories, and she uses that relationship and knowledge to help them grow their businesses. That might not make sense to you right now, as you are just starting this book, but I promise it will by the end.

I have had a front row seat as Beth has developed the art of Downline Whispering, all the while implementing many of the strategies I have learned from her. I KNOW many of the practices taught in this book helped me grow my organization to where we are today, and those practices are only going to help spring board our team onward from here. #todiamondandbeyond See, Beth not only taught me about stalking my downline, she taught me all about hashtags as well. Just wait until you read the first chapter, where you will begin to experience her love for the hashtag, too! I look forward to using this book as a tool for each new business member as they join our team. I love the simple steps Beth gives that show you EXACTLY how to look at the names on your computer screen and turn those into meaningful relationships, all without being overwhelmed! I encourage you to pull out a highlighter and get ready to mark this book up. You might think you are doing all you can "behind the scenes" of your business, but Beth will show you otherwise!

Communication, Motivation, Dedication, Positivity, Creativity, Trustworthiness. These are all words that you will see mentioned when you look up traits of great leaders. But to me, those words point to great CHARACTER. If we are to become leaders, then we must exemplify those characteristics. Beth Whicker not only shows us how to use these traits to help grow our teams, but she lives out those traits as well. There are so many pieces of the puzzle needed to build a successful organization, and this book is a major piece of that puzzle. Beth has written from the heart, focusing on the traits I mentioned above, and I for one am so thankful she is sharing her heart with all of Team Young Living.

Regardless of if you are leading a team of 10 members or 10,000, I believe you can benefit from learning how to be a Downline Whisperer. These daily, weekly and monthly practices are going to help take your business to the next level, all while building relationships with those on your team! Total win-win, right? I firmly believe the strategies she gives throughout this book will transform the way you look at your downline. Sit down, buckle up and get ready to enjoy the ride. You are well on your way to being a Downline Whispering pro!

~Mollie Cargill
Young Living Platinum Leader, Georgia

Part 1:
My Journey to Downline Whispering

"Hey, Guys!!!"

For those of you who don't know me, I'm Beth. Welcome to this crazy book on knowing and growing your team. The concept for this book has been on my heart and my mind for quite some time. However, it wasn't until recently that I decided to go out on a limb and make this dream become a reality. This didn't happen because I'm such an awesome "go-getter," but because I have some awesome friends who challenged me to apply myself and make this dream come true.

Has there ever been something in your life that you had a passion for, but fear kept you from pursuing it? What I'm talking about is an idea, concept or activity that is so amazing you know that it would help everyone if they would just listen, but you didn't try because you were too scared about what might happen?

In my opinion, one of the best movies Jim Carrey ever made was when he played Truman Burbank in *The Truman Show*. There was a particular scene in that movie that was very frustrating for me to watch.

When Truman was a child, his dad apparently died when they were out sailing. As a result of this traumatic event, Truman had an overwhelming fear of the water. He would never even touch the water; no way, no how. His fear was so overwhelming he wasn't even able to leave the island he was on because it required him to cross a long bridge. This fear, an irrational one at that, kept his world small and isolated even though he longed for freedom and adventure. That bridge was Truman's highway to liberation. Eventually, Truman was able to work through this fear and cross the bridge. Once he did, his world changed. What he thought he knew was not as it seemed. This allowed him to permanently leave the world that had entrapped him his entire life, all because he was able to overcome an irrational fear that he'd held for decades.

This may sound like you, and the reality is, it was me. This book was my "water." I refused to write this book for many months because I feared different things: people wouldn't want to read it, I wasn't an author, people don't want to hear anything I have to say…the list goes on and on. Yet here I am, writing a book that I hope will inspire many people on their journey because I know what I have to share has already transformed lives.

But I want to be real with you. As I sit here writing, the fear is creeping back in; "why would anyone want to read this book?" Immediately a sense of inadequacy nearly paralyzes me. I begin to think negatively and pessimistically, "Nobody is going to read a book by me. Who am I that anyone should listen?" After a couple of seconds of doubt, I snap back into reality and get a grip. I pray and ask for God's strength and clarity. He then refocuses my thoughts on all of the ways that what I'm about to share with you has significantly enhanced my business and my life. And I'm completely convinced that what I have discovered will not only help you, but it has the potential to revolutionize your business.

As we go on this adventure together, you will see that while this Network Marketing business has provided an amazing opportunity to provide financially for my family, more importantly, it has allowed me to build lasting friendships. However, building the business and building relationships didn't just happen by chance; it required work done with both my heart and my mind. In other words, I worked hard, and I worked intelligently in my building efforts. In fact, the principles and strategies that I'm going to share with you are the very ones that I still use as I continue to establish my business and form new relationships. So, I hope you're ready to be challenged, encouraged, and inspired because all of this and more is going to take place as you're reading *Downline Whispering: The art of knowing and growing your team.*

BETH WHICKER

Chapter 1: A Whisperer is Born

Jennifer Love Hewitt was a hot commodity at one point in her career. I can't lie, I was a fan of her work. Not so much the "I Know What You Did Last Summer" Jennifer Love Hewitt, more along the lines of the "Heartbreakers" Jennifer Love Hewitt. What can I say? I love a good, sappy, romantic movie. However, as I see it, in 2005 things began to go downhill for the beautiful brunette. It was during this year that the actress began a drama called "Ghost Whisperer." In this dramatic fantasy television show, Hewitt had the ability to listen to and communicate with the spirits of people who had recently died. Now, some people loved this series. However, I found it to be creepy, and if I'm honest, weird. I never even gave it a shot; though recently I have been intrigued to watch an episode or two. Interestingly, around that same time, there was another show that kicked off that was cut from a similar cloth – "Dog Whisperer." This show was centered around a man named Cesar. Cesar supposedly had an ability to communicate with dogs so, he used this "power" to help aid in the rehabilitation of canines who were suffering from various issues. Again, I found this show to be weird. As with the "Ghost Whisperer," I couldn't bring myself to watch. Little did I know that

I would eventually be mentioned in the same breath as these two shows. How? My friend, Rosy. Some friend, huh? Ha! Actually, she's pretty great. But she's the one who gave me a name that has come to define me and my business - the "Downline Whisperer."

If I had to define a "whisperer," it wouldn't be the definition of quietly talking in someone's ear. It would be more along the lines of the ability to communicate and interact with people on an intimate level. So in essence, a Whisperer is a person who excels at connecting, training and helping others succeed.

At first glance, Downline Whispering may seem like the strangest thing in the world. And to some, it may very well produce some awkward emotions and feelings; much like I felt thinking about those shows. But before you jump to any conclusions, I ask that you keep an open heart and mind. I truly believe what I'm about to tell you can completely revolutionize your business; just like it has mine. So, sit back, strap in, and get ready.

I want to start out by giving you a brief overview of what Downline Whispering is and how I got started on this journey, then we'll begin to unpack what it all means and how it can help your business specifically. To be completely honest, this entire whirlwind journey of being a Downline Whisperer began by accident, and it stemmed from the fact that I'm one of those bleeding-heart types. You know, the kind of person that would do almost anything for anyone. Naturally, this translated into my business. I felt that network marketing should be all about the people. This especially applies to Young Living, where we know our product works, and we just need to support and educate people on their journey.

Here's the thing, I didn't want to be someone who was just like, "Oh cool, my downline is growing!". I knew it needed to be more than that. I kept hearing everyone say that Young Living is a family and, in my experience, I knew family was supposed to care about each other. So, if I had a growing "family," I needed to be able to care for them. Even in my limited understanding of downlines, I knew they had the ability to grow exponentially. #sharingiscaring The question was, "how am I going let my growing downline know that I care for them?" The crux of the matter was how I could create an environment that truly feels like a family? In my mind, the answer was easy. I would be a complete and total stalker. HA! I get it. It even sounds creepy to me as I'm sitting here typing it out. You know that feeling I got when I thought about those weird shows - "Ghost Whisperer" and "Dog Whisperer"? Yeah, I was becoming the very thing I despised. I just didn't realize it. But it gets worse; I want you to be weird, too. I want you to become a Downline Whisperer just like me.

Now, understand, I didn't immediately realize that what I was doing was something that many people weren't doing with their own downlines. I just assumed everyone else was doing it. I mean, how else could you care for these people unless you were actively involved? But you know what they say about assuming – if you don't know, I'll let you look that one up on your own. #notappropriate #movingon

The light bulb about the uniqueness of what I was doing didn't come on until my friend, Rosy, uttered those haunting words to me, "ahhh, friend, you are the Downline Whisperer!"

I was stunned. "What do you mean, I'm the Downline Whisperer?"

She then proceeded to tell me exactly what she thought and how she felt about what I was doing. She had no idea how to do what it was I had been doing and, to her knowledge, she had never heard of anyone else doing it. Now, some people, because of their personality, are more inclined to stalk their downline and Virtual Office, but she wasn't one of those people. She desperately wanted and needed to be taught how to do it. You'll hear her side of the story towards the end of this book, so if this freaks you out, you'll want to check out her chapter. #shehidfromherVO #truestory After my initial shock wore off, I began teaching Rosy how to "whisper" to her downline. And so it began.

I get it, many of you may already do some of the things I am going to talk about. DUDE! You're already ahead of the game, and that's kind of a huge deal. My prayer, however, is that this book gives you and your team the tools to easily replicate successfully managing your downlines. Remember, it's about family. It's about knowing your people personally so you can accurately, competently, and quickly care for them. I know what it's like to look at your computer screen, staring blankly, while saying 'WHAT THE HECK DO I DO NOW?' I want you to know there's hope. You can effectively and efficiently care for those in your downline to the point that it's more than just a business; it can feel like a *family*. And that's what I want to share with you in this book.

Chapter 2: My Story

Sneak Peek

Have you ever been in a situation that allowed you to have a sneak peek at something? I can vividly remember all of my pregnancies. I was like a kid at Christmastime. There was absolutely no way I was going to be able to wait until the baby was born to find out whether it was a boy or girl. I had to know as soon as possible. I made sure my sonogram appointments were set up well in advance, and I prayed that the baby would be in the right position so we could "figure things out." You see, a sonogram is a type of a sneak peek. They "pull back the curtain" and enable you to see something that other people haven't seen. And this is exactly what I want to do for you. I want to give you a sneak peek into my life; a look at something not everyone has seen.

Why would I want to "pull back the curtain"? Authenticity. One of my personal core values is being genuine. In other words, I want to be real. In order for me to be who I'm created to be, I must be transparent with other people; I need to let other people see who I am. You need to know about my journey. Knowing my journey will prepare you to hear my heart as you travel through this book. So, before we go full on crazy into stalking, I want to tell you about me. #herewego

My Crazy Life

"Hey, guys!!!!!!"

I know, I know, I already said this at the beginning of the book. But here's the thing, this is me. If you've ever seen any of my videos, you know this is my go-to introduction. But I'm sure there are going to be people reading this who don't have any idea who I am. For those of you who don't know me, I want us to become friends. So let me tell you who I am. As I said earlier, my name is Beth, and to be honest, I really shouldn't even be writing a book. I mean, gosh, what type of life is this? I'll share more on that a little later. I've been married to Jake, {the sexiest, most amazing man in the whole wide world} since 2004. I am also blessed to be a mother. If you follow me, you know I've said that becoming a mother beautifully devastated me. You see, I have four absolutely incredible children. I am a birth mom to a gorgeous 15-year-old girl, and God's hand of blessing has been all over that situation. She has an amazing mom and dad who love her, care for her, and train her up in the Lord. #adoptionrocks I also have three crazy kids with Jake: Halee - 12, Karis - 10 and Jett - 9. I attempt to homeschool these munchkins; only time will tell how I've done. #helpmeJesus As for who I am outside of my family, you don't have to be around me long to understand that I love hugs and I love coffee. I also love, Love, LOVE my Converse and I love to dream big - because my sweet husband taught me how. I have been a diehard Redskins fan since I was 5 years old #HTTR, and for the last 2 years, I have had the honor of being a radio show host on FreeThinkers Radio. Now you pretty much know everything you need to know about me. #ifeellikewearefriends #nowsyourchancetorun

Let's delve into my Young Living story a bit more. In 2013, we lived in a small beach town in Florida where my husband was planting a church. If you know anything about this you understand that he didn't make much money, so I needed to work in order to help with the bills. I worked three jobs – and we still qualified for government assistance. These jobs could not have been any more different from each other. I worked at a pawn shop, on a sandwich truck, and I cleaned a beach house. I did all of these because we needed money. I was blessed to have those jobs in an area that was hit hard economically; this part of Florida lost approximately 30% of their population in the previous 10 years. This was due, in large part, to a lack of employment opportunities; most everyone moved elsewhere to find a job. So, I was fortunate to find three different occupations that I really enjoyed. The cherry on top was that I had lots of fun working for some amazing bosses who taught me some crucial lessons of entrepreneurship. But at the end of the day, we were still significantly struggling financially.

As all of this was taking place, I was desperately looking for something to assist me on my health journey. During this search, I had become very intrigued by essential oils. I definitely didn't know why they were "essential," all I knew is that the Bible talked about them, so they had to help in some way. I was interested. I was SO interested in fact, that I tried quite a few different oil brands and companies. #disappointed Nothing seemed to work. I was really discouraged. Then, I heard about Young Living Essential Oils through a friend of a friend, who later became my enroller. But, since I had tried so many different brands, without experiencing much success, I was bound and determined to research as much as I could before I made any type of purchase. I Googled Young Living. I went on Facebook and stalked them. I even joined several different Facebook groups to find out as much as I could. I'm telling you, I was adamant about gathering as much intel as possible before I made a financial commitment. #iwasntplaying Plus, I was a huge skeptic. I was even a little ugly about it; you can ask my enroller someday. I needed to be convinced, and it wasn't going to be easy. #stubborn Finally, after weeks and weeks of research, I had seen enough. I was ready to take the plunge. There was just one problem: my husband. I mean, he's not a problem #wellsometimes but it was obvious that he wasn't going to have any part in me buying oils; 1) because the other brands didn't work and 2) we were so strapped for cash. So, I concocted a brilliant plan - at least it was brilliant in my mind. I would put a little extra money away each month, without Jake knowing, until I had saved enough to purchase the Premium Starter Kit. And that's exactly what I did. Being very, very sneaky, ummm, I mean discerning, I was able to save up enough money to purchase the kit. So, on the very last day of November 2013, I saw that same mutual friend post about getting a free bottle of oil with a kit purchase. Who doesn't like free? #ilikefree I jumped all in and bought my kit with a free 15ml bottle of Orange essential oil. #letsgetiton #orangeforallwomen #bestdayofmyhusbandslife #hejustdidnotknowityet

Coming Clean

As I'm sure you can figure out, eventually I was going to have to come clean and let Jake know that I bought this kit from a total stranger - online. #funnybutnot About two weeks after I purchased the kit, I let him know what I had done. He wasn't mad, he just didn't understand why I spent that money on some "snake oils." And yes, he called them snake oils for at least 6 months. Don't worry; he's obsessed now. #peppermintdidit Finally, I had everything lined up. I knew I was on my way to personal health, purpose, and abundance. Well, minus the abundance part. One thing was for sure; the oils were for personal use only. In no way, shape, or form was I interested in doing this as a business. Absolutely not! No way! Not Me! You weren't going to catch me dead doing another one of those "MLM scams." Oh yes, we had done plenty of "those types" of businesses before. We knew people who were very successful in Network Marketing but, after many failed attempts, both Jake and I made a vow to never do anything like that again. #heckno

Wearing Me Down

Ha! As you can tell, my resistance didn't last long at all. Which is weird, because you've got to understand something about me; I'm a stubborn girl. My dad was a "lifer" in the Marines. He taught me to be steadfast and resolute in the decisions that I make. When you decide on something, stand by it. Don't let anyone push you around. Don't let other people bully you into something you don't want to do. I was set in my persistence; I was not going to do the business. Remember, Jake and I had made the decision to never do an MLM again. #freakinscams That choice, forged in the fire of being reared in a Marine household, lasted all of 2 months. And for the life of me, I couldn't understand what was happening. I felt so weak. Why was my willpower failing? I didn't want to do this business. But here I was being drawn into this crazy adventure called Young Living Essential Oils. What changed my mind, you ask? I fell in love with the oils. #theychangedeverything And, if you've ever been in love, you know that love will do some crazy things.

An Accidental Journey

My husband is a huge movie buff. Being married to him for 13 years means he has definitely rubbed off on me. Even though I am a total #extrovert, there are times I love just having a night at the house watching a good movie. But I am very picky with my movies. I'm sort of a movie snob if you will. One day he asked me to watch The Hobbit with him. I said, "Uhh Nope. Not happening." But he tricked me. And, of course, I fell for it. I don't even remember how it all happened; he probably bribed me with Starbucks. #moviesnob #coffeesnob So, I ended up watching the first movie in the series. I didn't care for it. Let's just get that out of the way. What I do remember, though, is that it was referred to as "An Unexpected Journey." The main character, Bilbo Baggins, was caught off guard by a charming wizard named Gandalf. Reluctantly, Bilbo entered a fun and adventurous journey that led him to majestic places and into dangerous situations, all the while, making new friends along the way. There's a point to me bringing up this movie. #promise You see, this is how I feel about my journey with Young Living. #unexpectedjourney #thankful

In fact, it was more accidental than anything else. You might think, "how in the world could you accidentally start a business?" Well, I'm so glad you asked. Let me tell you how. After I began to use the oils consistently, as I mentioned earlier, I absolutely fell in love with them. I just loved the way they made me feel. And being an empath, #feelallthefeels, I wanted other people to feel the same way I felt. #bleedingheart Naturally, I started telling my friends and family about how these oils were positively affecting my life. Add to this the fact that I am an "oversharer" - and you had the perfect storm. By the way, an oversharer is someone who puts all of their personal business out there for the world to know. #idontevencare Just ask my husband, or any of my family for that matter. They just love when I word vomit everywhere. #notreally #theystillloveme. I digress. This is why I say it was an "accidental journey." I didn't have this grand scheme of how I was going to start a business and make it successful. #areyoukidding That thought never crossed my mind. Let me tell you how I viewed myself: I wasn't anything special. I didn't have a college degree or any special skill set - unless you call dropping out of college, "special." But little did I know that my "oversharing" could actually be used as a skill. Usually, I was getting in trouble from word vomiting, but oversharing had its benefits. By putting all of my personal business out there, people knew what these oils meant to me. As I learned to harness my "oversharing" I informed others about how the oils had supported my body's systems and helped my family in many ways. As a result, I found myself on the verge of selling the Premium Starter Kit. #almostbutnotquite

When I say on the verge, what I mean is that I had people chomping at the bit to get their own oils. The problem was I had no clue what I was doing. Literally, I tried everything I could to NOT sell them a kit. #iwasadummy #hellomcfly I told several people, "just log into my account and buy whatever you want." I'm pretty sure that's not allowed, but again, I had NO IDEA what I had gotten myself into. So, I just did what made the most sense in my mind. Thankfully, I have some persistent friends. A few of them opened my eyes to the fact that I might have a real business opportunity at my fingertips. #lightbulb Finally, I agreed with them. So, sometime in January of 2014, I made it official; I started my unexpected journey into this oily biz.

The Unlikely Entrepreneur

This is how my Young Living ride began. However, it wasn't without its bumps. From the get-go, Jake said he didn't mind me doing the business, as long as his name wasn't in anyway associated with it. Not only did he not believe in the oils, but he didn't believe in the business. Remember, we had a strong impression that all MLMs were scams. Despite any of the perceived or real obstacles, I found my business growing. By the end of the very first month, my team was 4 members deep. It was a very modest beginning, but for me, it was extremely exciting; I had my own little, legitimate business, I was really doing this!!! Could it be? Was I an entrepreneur? Why, yes. Yes, I was! At least I certainly thought I was. From that point on, I put my head down and started working this thing with all I had. By the end of February, our little tight-knit team had grown to 28 avid oil users; a handful of which decided to jump in and do the business. I had now hit the rank of Executive. #dingdingding With my organization growing more rapidly than I had ever imagined, I knew I needed to do something that would enable me to accurately and efficiently handle all of the change. I didn't get into this by thinking small; I was dreaming big. I wanted to keep the momentum going so I could eventually hit Silver, Gold, Platinum, and beyond. So, I did the only thing I knew to do. A thing I was already pretty good at - I stalked my downline. #creeperalert

I can tell you this much; Downline Whispering worked for me. It helped my team achieve the rank of Platinum in 15 months, and it's on the verge of helping me climb the next mountain – leading a Diamond organization. But, again, it's about more than the ranks and the money. Downline Whispering has enabled me to build real relationships with the people in my team. I can remember Jake asking me who some of my closest friends were. You know what I told him? Most of them were people from my Young Living business. One of my personally enrolled was a referral whom I had never met before. Not only is she almost a Gold leader now, but she is also one of my closest friends. #thatsahugedeal I know it works. It's worked for me, and I've seen it help many others with their businesses and relationships alike. Downline Whispering has been an invaluable tool for me. It's taken me this far and I honestly believe, if you're willing to put in the time and effort in learning, it will do the same for you.

Embrace Your Story

I'm not naïve to think that my story is the only one of its kind. Sure, the details are unique, but I know for a fact that there are many others who have found this to be an accidental business. On the other hand, some of you saw the awesome potential from the moment someone shared with you, and you jumped right in.

Every situation is incredible! That's what makes your story so powerful; don't ever shy away from it. Your story is part of your unique journey. And you, too, can use that story as you're helping others in their adventure. All of these things add up, and they play a crucial role in the "why" and "how" of your business.

Encouragement and Inspiration

I know, without a doubt, that our stories make all the difference in the world. They can encourage, inspire, and assist other people as they're "writing" their own story. And, guess what? The people you're inspiring just may turn around and do the same for you. But in order to encourage and impact, you've got to be open; you've got to share your story. Sharing may be difficult for you. You may be a very private person. I'd encourage you to work at opening up your life to someone else. You may not "put it all out there" on Social Media like I do, but I'd encourage and challenge you to pick one person you trust and begin sharing your story with them. I promise you; you will see good come from it. You will start to see changes happening in your own life. On top of that, you never know what it might do in the life of the other person. This is the real reason I would like to tell you how I've managed my growing business. Hopefully, by hearing what God has done in and through my life, it will challenge, encourage, and inspire you. Then, I want you to be empowered to go out and make things happen.

Now, you might be wondering, "Why in the world should I listen to this weirdo?" I get it, I wonder the same thing at times, too. You know...when I talk to myself. #weirdo The only thing I can say is this; Downline Whispering has been transformational for my business. Because of this, I've had the opportunity to speak with teams from all over the world about what I do, and they've all had a similar refrain, "I didn't know I should, let alone know I could, do ALL of this with my downline. With this information, I feel like I can really start helping my members and my business builders more effectively." So, not only has this tactic worked for me, but I have seen it work time and time again for many other Young Living leaders. And this is really my heartbeat; helping others. I desire to be the best leader I can be to those whom God has put in my life through this business. But I could not have accomplished this without being able to know my people, and Downline Whispering was the method by which I was able to achieve this. I don't just want to know where people are in my organization; I want to know THEM. I want to understand who the leaders are, if individuals are set to rank up or maintain rank, if they've enrolled new members, and so much more. These are all really important things you need to be aware of as your organization grows. It shows you care about the people under you. In just a little bit I'm going to walk you through some practical tips to help you become a Downline Whisperer. #letswhispertogether

The Biz

I do understand that you're not reading this book simply for "the feels." You want some concrete information that you can use to enhance your business. I want that for you, too. Over the course of these pages, I'll be sharing with you how I personally choose to hit ranks, build my downline legs, and more. I'm not writing this because I think I have it all together; believe me, I don't. #iamahotmess #askmyclosestfriends But I do believe I have found something that works, and I've seen it work for others. What I'm going to share isn't the only way to build your business. But, by letting you know what I've learned, you might see an idea or two that helps you as you're looking to better manage your organization; relationally and/or structurally. As we're all a part of a business family, I want to help us all to be as successful as possible.

The Heart of a Whisperer

Before we get into the specifics, I need you to grasp something: if you don't care about building personal relationships with your team, Downline Whispering will be of no benefit to you. The entire premise of Downline Whispering is interpersonal relationships. I firmly believe that learning WHO your team members are is more important than knowing WHAT your team members are doing. When I say I "know" my team members, I'm speaking of more than just knowing their names; it means I know their stories. I should be able to answer questions like: what is their "why," do they have a family, why did they start using oils? If you care about questions like these, and I think you should, then you're on your way to being a Downline Whisperer yourself. I firmly believe that your downline will not grow if you, as the leader, don't keep tabs on your team. And here's the thing, you can do this all from your Virtual Office and on Social Media – which we'll talk about in detail later. Granted, there are some teams who have succeeded despite this family atmosphere, but those seem to be the exception and not the rule. So, Downline Whispering requires you step out of your comfort zone and connect with the people on your team on a personal level. #letsdothis #HeartOfTheWhisperer

You've Been Warned

If you're just starting your business, Downline Whispering is an amazing way for you to kick things off. Let me warn you; it will take a lot of patience, hard work, and determination up front to learn the process. But as you become more familiar with it, it will eventually become second nature. As you become more proficient at Downline Whispering, even as your business grows, you'll notice that you are able to put less effort into this skill because it will be completely natural. So when you hit a thousand (or two or three or ten thousand) members, you won't even think twice about sailing right through the process of whispering to your downline. #easypeasy. However, if you already have a thriving organization, I won't sugar coat it, Downline Whispering will be more difficult for you to master. Why? It's simply a numbers game. Stalking your Virtual Office with a downline of ten thousand members is much more daunting than stalking a downline with two-hundred members. If your organization is bigger, it will take you a little longer to get into the groove of this art form, but you will get there. Don't worry. Just keep at it. Be consistent, and you'll be cruising as you stalk your downline like a pro!

Don't be Scared

At least at first, Downline Whispering can, and probably will be intimidating; especially as your downline grows. If I could give you one piece of advice it would be this; don't be scared. Have no fear. Fear is a freakin' liar. It's a mirage. It will keep you from doing and experiencing things that could be life changing. #stepout Years ago, there was an apparel company that was very popular. They made a lot of money from their slogan – No Fear! They had shirts, hats, pants, accessories, and the like. Their entire business was centered around the idea of not letting fear hold you back from experiencing the adventures life had for you. That's what I want you to do right now; get dressed in your "No Fear" gear. Downline Whispering can be life changing for you and your business. Punch fear in the face and experience the adventures this business has for you. #areyouready

Life Changing?

Okay Beth, C'mon! We are talking about something that's supposed to help with my business. How in the world can this possibly be "life changing"? Let's be honest; this life isn't about the money you make or the stuff you have; it's about the relationships you build. If you were to become extremely successful and earn lots of money in this business, but you didn't have anyone to share that with, what have you really accomplished? That's what Downline Whispering is all about; building a business while building relationships. Sure, Downline Whispering isn't the only way to have a successful business, but I do believe it's one of the best formulas for building your business while simultaneously building relationships. I think this process beautifully weaves the two together into a masterpiece that you'll be proud of, both personally and professionally.

A Business and Relationship Builder

How does Downline Whispering create such a masterpiece? By becoming familiar with this process, you can truly get to KNOW your people. After all, how can you treat people as family if you have no idea who they are or what's going on in their lives? This one fact, for me, is enough in and of itself to learn how to stalk my downline. However, Downline Whispering will help you with more than just knowing your people; it will assist you with accurately and effectively keeping track of your growing business. Don't get discouraged. Just be prepared to dig in and work. As you learn, you'll get better. As you practice the right things, you'll become more comfortable with your stalking skills. I'm confident you'll see the benefits sooner rather than later. But you can't be scared. In order to be an effective "Downline Whisperer," you need to be comfortable with scrolling through and seeing your teams' kit sales, recognizing the people placed under you, tracking each of your business legs, asking personal questions, and much more. These are things that, at first, will seem overwhelming, but through training, you are sure to master. #someofmyfavoritethings

Organized Chaos

Sometimes, when I have a chance to sit back and actually think about what I'm doing, it all seems a bit chaotic. And, I must admit that if you're not careful, Downline Whispering could easily spiral out of control. But, as long as you're taking things step by step, everything will be fine. Now, I'm not saying everything will be smooth and easy. To be honest, it will probably still be hectic; maybe even chaotic. But when you understand the method to my madness, it will be more of an organized chaos than an outright crazy person chaos. So, let's look at the method to my madness.

Chapter 3: Time to Build

One at a Time

When I first started building my downline, I was at a loss; I wasn't sure the best way to go about it. I knew I wanted to set myself up for long-term success, but I wasn't sure how I would accomplish that. So, I did the same thing I did when I was thinking about purchasing my kit; I started researching. I wanted to know how other successful entrepreneurs built their organizations. After a lot of thought, much research, and several heated arguments with my husband, I settled on a method. I chose to build my organization by working on my first 2 legs; then I would move on, one leg at a time. After I felt the first legs were firmly established, I quickly moved to my 3rd leg. Once again, when I felt it was solid, I moved on to my 4th. At the time of this writing, I am working on my 5th leg, while keeping an eye out for my 6th. You only need 6 legs to hit the highest rank in Young Living: Royal Crown Diamond. Many other successful leaders chose to build all 6 legs at the same time; which worked for them and is another great way to grow your business. In fact, this is one of the reasons my husband and I argued; he felt like I should build 6 legs at one time. It was important to me to structure my business the way I did because my husband had just finished planting a church and we needed the extra income. Hitting rank quickly not only provided some much needed financial flexibility it also inspired me and my team to keep growing. This meant that my check was larger, quicker and that my leaders were VESTED and more likely not to quit. So, although I may have stunted my growth a little bit in one aspect, in another aspect I solidified my team; they are along for this ride WITH me. It's encouraging to know that I'm not growing alone. I suggest talking with your enroller or upline and your spouse/confidant to figure out the best method for you.

Sharing the business

In order to grow, you need to focus on helping others get started with this amazing business opportunity. This is exactly what I did from the get go, and I've had a decent amount of success. Around 70% of the awesome people who buy a kit from me end up jumping into the business. I know the first question I'm going to get is, "HOW did you flip approximately 70% to the business side?" Let's take a little time to discuss several strategies that I used to transition people from oil users to oil sharers.

First, if people are already on ER, let them know that they can get their oils paid for. Who doesn't want to get a check that pays for their monthly obsession? #yesplease It really is that simple.

Second, if people are already sharing about their oils on Facebook or in person, or if non-business builders are adding friends to your members' group, it's so simple to pop in and let them know that they are already doing what a business person does - SHARING.

Third, reach out to people who have a kit and have a large following, I mean that's self-explanatory, right? People listen to them on a blog or social media. Highlight for them the potential they have right at their fingertips. And I mean, who doesn't want to make a couple of extra bucks?

But what about presenting the business to someone like a family member or close friend? I did this with my sister. She really loved the oils, even her husband was using them, but she didn't want to take it out of their family budget (she has like a bunch of little kids). DUH. So I approached her like this: "Hey, I know you love oils, and I'd love to help you start getting your oils paid for. Wanna give it a try?" It's super important that you are confident when you share, even if you're scared to death. Some people truly need some additional income, and guess what? It's so easy to share about these amazing oils because they WORK! So share with the world, people!

My sweet friend, Jerri-Anne Joyner, offers the business to everyone who buys a kit. Yep, you heard me. EVERYONE. I have really learned a lot from her because she loves people enough to let them know there's an income opportunity. What's the worst they can say? No! The thing about it, she's had some people who would have never done the business without her informing them. How many other people out there are like that? They're just waiting for you to let them know that there is a business opportunity waiting for them.

Here's some bonus material because I love you. #score Mary Young once told a group that the oils sell themselves because they work. All you've got to do is let people experience them. The fact that you are willing to let people try your oils is huge. If people know that you care about THEM, their health and their well-being...many will want to join you on this journey because they see that the oils work, the company is legit, and the community is real. In other words, they get to see what the oils, the company, and the community have done for you. #thatsabigdeal

Strategic Placement

Since I wanted to do what I could to support my team, I worked hard at placing new enrollees under them. Because we were working together, my first two legs grew, and I hit Silver rather quickly and qualified for Silver in 6 (now Si6). I found that my numbers started multiplying and knew now, more than ever, stalking my downline was a necessity for keeping this unforeseen, booming business straight. So, I put my plan into action. I would start by going through each leg to make sure each person was building their business legs by restructuring (using strategic placement) correctly. I also wanted to verify that my business builders had at least 100pv so they wouldn't miss out on their commissions and that their Essential Rewards (ER) were set up, so they were earning points toward free products. Finally, I wanted to know if anyone was close to hitting or maintaining their rank. I did all of this not only because I wanted to help them, but I wanted to encourage them and celebrate with them along the way.

By May of 2014, I was a Silver team leader with 165 members in my organization. Fast forward to the end of November, and I was a Gold with 827 people on my team. And because I was faithfully "stalking" my downline, I can honestly say that I knew all of my business members by name. On top of that, I knew where most of my team's members were located. This was so important to me because, as I've said, I wanted each person to know that they were more than just a monthly order; they were people who I wanted to have a relationship with in some way.

#protip

You need to be very aware of something should you choose to build your business one leg at a time. Prepping for the next leg does not mean you ignore all of the other legs; you simply place new kit sales in the leg you're trying to build. If you neglect the other legs because you're too focused on the one leg you're trying to build, you'll make those in your other legs feel like you don't need them.

#becareful #avoidthisgrowingpain

Chapter 4: It's the Relationships - Being Others Focused

Let's talk about selfishness vs. selflessness. It can be very easy to get caught up in your own advancement, but I'd caution you to guard against that. Why? Because your TEAM's SUCCESS is YOUR SUCCESS. If you follow me at all on social media, I'm sure you've figured out that I love and follow Jesus. #ihopethatshows Because of this fact, I believe that what the Bible says is true. But the Bible isn't just something to know; it's something to live. In Philippians 2:4 it says, "Don't look out only for your own interests, but take an interest in others, too." So, when I say the Bible is to be "lived out," that means it's something that should transcend every area of my life. I don't have a separate family life, church life, and business life when it comes to my relationship with Jesus; He is my life. So, my business is informed by this relationship. And, because of what Philippians 2:4 says, I want to be just as concerned about others as I am for myself; whether they can benefit me or not. #careaboutpeople

What does it look like to be "others focused?" I'll talk about this more in depth a little later, but let me give you a taste. When you do an act of service for someone, it shows them you're thinking about them, and you value the relationship you have with them. It's doing things like sending "happy mail" - putting a postcard, card, or gift in the mail to someone on your team. I'm sure you know what it's like to get something in the mail; it makes you feel good to know that the person cared enough to do it.

Another thing that really makes people feel like they are part of the community is celebrating their successes in front of the rest of the team. When someone sells their first kit, is teaching a rockin' class or ranks up for the first time - CELEBRATE. #letsparty Post about them in your Facebook business group. Let others know what they have done and how proud you are of them. This is probably one of my favorite things to do, and the rest of the team is SO inspired and cheers each other on. It's a big online party!

Last but not least, I highly recommend praying for your business, your members, your business builders, and your potential (and even non-potential) kit buyers. This is a true form of selflessness. Prayer isn't just about seeking blessings for your business; it helps keep you focused on what really matters – people.

These are just some of the steps you can take to keep your business others focused. Trust me, if you aren't focused on the people now, if and when you become successful, you'll easily lose sight of what really matters and then the business will become something it should not be; all about the money and the rank. #keepthemainthingthemainthing

Crossline Relationships

Crossline relationships and collaboration is my jam. I have found them to be extremely rewarding and freeing. Why? Because with these relationships, it is truly about wanting other people to succeed. I don't make money from their success. Their growth doesn't directly impact my business. We're simply there to help each other in this oily life. Just make sure it's a two-way street and that you're collaborating. #giveandtake Here's the beautiful thing about Young Living, and network marketing companies in general; if others are successful, it, in turn, helps you to be successful. I have learned so much from my amazing crossline friendships. Their strategies and tips have helped to excite and empower my team as we're on this journey. #butwait #theresmore If this is true of crossline relationships how much more is it true of the people in your organization? The entire design of Young Living's business structure is one of others' successes being your success. If your only concern is YOU, then your team is going to see that. It will be very apparent that you are only about yourself. The result is that your team, your oily *family*, will feel hurt and neglected by your selfishness. I'm telling you, I have seen it happen. People who are successful at the expense of others may, for a time, be successful, but eventually, the cat will be out of the bag. People don't want to work with someone who's only about themselves. It's your responsibility to help your people be as successful as they can possibly be.

In the Know

There's another aspect of focusing on others; knowing who's close to ranking up. If my business builders are close to ranking up to the next level, it's my responsibility to know that. Once I know who's close, I can then reach out and try to help them in any way I can. But, I don't know what I don't know. How can I know what someone needs from me unless I ask them? And how will I know to ask them unless I see they're close to hitting rank? And how will I know they're close to hitting rank unless I have kept track of their business through the Virtual Office? Are ya pickin' up what I'm puttin' down? #getitgotitgood This is the importance of Downline Whispering. It enables me to keep track of every one of these aspects so that I can be "in the know." Also, it shows my people that I care enough to pay attention, to know where they are in their business building and to reach out and help where needed.

Knowledge + Action

I've heard it said that leaders aren't people who can just identify problems. After all, can't anyone identify a problem? Rather, according to Pastor Nic Burleson, "leaders are people who can identify solutions." I want each and every one of us to be a leader. I want us to be people who identify solutions and not just problems. Solutions are action based steps to help people achieve success. Specifically, in our context, solutions are action based steps to help each other be successful in our businesses. We should want to find solutions to help our people hit that next rank, draw in that skeptic, develop financial freedom, or whatever else it may be that they need and want. See, it's not enough to know what someone needs; I've got to act on that knowledge. Once I know what my people need, I must to go out and do. This is what's called the "follow through." It's me knowing and doing what is necessary to help my people. That's what family does. That's what leaders do. You stay "in the know," then, based on that knowledge, you get involved when needed. Being a Downline Whisperer isn't knowledge or action; it's both. You need to know, then act. Without both tools in your tool belt, you won't be effective, and your team will suffer. #findsolutions

#protip

At the end of the month go through each business leg and see who is close to ranking up. I pull up *My Organization* and go through it one leg at a time, looking at each business builder to see if they're close to ranking up. I love looking through all of my legs, seeing their names, and knowing that the numbers represent people. If you've grown to 100 members or more, it will take more time. But as you do this consistently, it will become second nature. Also, train your downline to do this. As you're learning, help them to learn with you. As they learn, you'll find yourself becoming more comfortable while needing to do it less and less. As your team becomes comfortable, they will be able to do much of the work themselves. I still go through my entire downline at least once a week. With over 3600 members, almost 600 of which are at least tinkering with the business side, I'm just now starting to have trouble recognizing some of the names of the newer business builders. #makesmesad #butitsgood Downline Whispering enables me to stay knowledgeable, ask questions and empower my people.

Reproduction

My husband has been a pastor for six years. He's passionate about teaching people and helping them understand the Bible. One of the key tenets of Christianity is to lead people who can turn around and lead others. So, one of the things that he says and teaches constantly is that we need to "reproduce reproducers." In other words, Christians should be leading people who are leading people who are leading people; they should be reproducing themselves in others. People should understand that they need to replace themselves. A church cannot and should not be dependent on just a few people; everyone needs to be involved. But this will only happen as people are reproducing themselves; leading others in what you're learning so they can in turn go and do the same thing. This is what truly frees people up. When everyone is taking their share of responsibility that means everyone is sharing the load equally. And this allows people to "stay in their lane." Let's face it; some people are better at some things than you are. They need to be doing those things so you can stick to the things in which you're gifted and talented. #nooneisgoodateverything This creates a well-oiled machine. #punintended

This suggestion may seem a little odd to you, but I think we should be doing the same thing in our business. We should be making ourselves replaceable.

I know, I know, you think I'm cray cray. Like, "Beth, why in the world would I do that?" Well, we should do that for the same reasons I mentioned above; you cannot do this thing on your own. When I first started stalking my downline, I was doing it every single day. #legit Things were much different then; my team was small enough that I could comfortably handle Downline Whispering all on my own. At this point in my career, however, if I were to try to do this same thing, it would be too much. I would not have time to do the things I want to do and in which I'm gifted. If I were to try to do it all on my own, I think it would end up eventually killing any motivation I have to make this thing succeed. So, what I did was work hard at training my leaders to be Downline Whisperers themselves. I reproduced reproducers. Now that they're proficient at stalking their own teams, I don't need to do it nearly as extensively as I used to. That has freed me up to focus on things like stalking my personal enrollments, investing in developing more leaders, and writing this book. As you can see, reproducing reproducers has given me the ability to concentrate on things I need and want to do. I'm still constantly Whispering, but nowhere near the level I was when I first started. This goes to show the importance of not just relying on yourself to be "The Downline Whisperer," but reproducing this skill in others so now you have multiple Downline Whisperers in the family. Trust me; you want it this way. #youwillthankmelater

Conclusion

You've had a chance to hear my heart and a piece of my story. My journey has shown that the benefits of stalking your downline and loving your people can have an amazing effect on your business and your life. At this point, we are going to make a transition. We are going to spend the rest of our time looking at the best practices for Downline Whispering. If you aren't naturally a Downline Whisperer, just take it slow and write everything down, it will become more natural to you as you practice. I'm SO excited that you're taking the time to work at growing yourself and your business. Please know that I'm praying for you as you continue to develop into a Downline Whispering pro yourself.

Part 2: Best Practices

Now it's time to get to the meat. This is the application section. These are the things you can actively do to help you and your team grow. Through a lot of trial and error, I have learned some valuable lessons. I've seen what you should be doing, as well as things that should be avoided. I've broken down the practices of Downline Whispering into three categories: daily, weekly, and monthly practices.

What this means is that there are some things that are so crucial to your business that you need to be doing them every single day. Other things, while important, are not a daily necessity; you can practice these weekly. And still others, you should save for once a month. Why have I broken them down like this? Put it this way, if you were to do all of these every day, you might end up bald like my husband. #lessstressnotmore #allthecedarwood #androsemary BUT, if you learn to do these daily, weekly and monthly whisperings, you'll get to enjoy your lovely head of hair for many years to come. So, without further ado, let's dig in.

Chapter 5: Daily Whisperings

When you think about making changes in your own life, what do you tend to think about? Most people tend to think about holistic changes that should take place for their lives to be better. Admittedly, you may need to make sweeping changes for some things like mental, emotional, spiritual, or physical health to take place – if you're a diabetic what you eat must change immediately, or you will endanger your life. However, massive changes are not usually necessary or effective for lasting, real world benefits. In his book "The Compound Effect," Darrin Hardy teaches the importance of making small changes daily. When you practice these daily changes consistently for thirty, forty-five, or sixty days, eventually they will form a new, good habit. Then, after you have mastered that one, small change, you can then move on to another small change. Once you've practiced this habit for a consistent amount of time to form another good habit, it will be time for another small change. As these changes begin to compound one on top of the other, you begin to see dramatic life change. A small change added to another small change added to another small change eventually results in big change. Thus, the compound effect. In the same way, there are small things you can and should be doing every single day with your downline that will produce drastic results within your organization. So, let's talk about these "Daily Whisperings" that I do to help maintain my growing team.

#protip

Grab a pen and paper and get ready to write. As you're starting this process, you may feel as though smoke is going to start billowing out of your ears. Don't freak out; this is where the pen and paper become your lifeline. It very well may be overwhelming, but it will get easier as you practice these small changes every single day - the compound effect.

Prospects

First things first. There is an awesome, newer feature in the Virtual Office called the *Prospects*. You can find it as a tab in "My Organization." Young Living has made it super easy to find. This report is a list of enrollees who provided their contact information, but did not complete their enrollment. This report is provided so that you may assist the person in completing their enrollment. Far too many times these people are lost in the virtual world, and no one ever capitalizes on the information they've provided. Once you've found their contact info, you can and should reach out to them. What I would recommend is simply shooting them a personal note:

Hey, 'Sally' – I saw that you tried signing up, but haven't yet completed your enrollment. Were you looking at other products besides your kit or did you get stuck? Please let me know how I can help!!

This is a super easy way to connect with a prospect without pounding on their door and scaring them away by being overly pushy. If you are doing this every single day, you are creating a stop-gap and making sure people aren't falling through the cracks. Plus, you're letting them know you care about them; you're taking the time and making an effort to confirm they are taken care of. Whether that ends up in any type of sale or not, what you've done is shown that you care more about people than money. That speaks volumes to those who are already on your team and those who will eventually join your team. Think about how you'd feel if you were that "prospect." If someone reached out to you in that manner, chances are, if you decided to purchase or do the business, you'd respect that person as a leader and want to be on their team. See how a little thing can make a big impact? I'm telling you, it works.

Daily Practice Number 1:
Reading your Prospects Report.

Retail Customers

Next up, let's go to your reports, which can be found in the Virtual Office under "My Organization" and check out "Retail Customers." This will show you anyone that has signed up solely as a retail customer. Personally, I never, EVER sign up retail customers if I can help it. I do this purposely because, for me, I think it's a waste of money. I believe the Premium Starter Kit is the best, most valuable purchase Young Living provides, so I try to steer away from signing up retail customers. However, some people want to sign up as retail regardless, so I'll walk you through how to let them know about the pros and cons of being a retail customer. Here's how it might go:

"Hey 'Kathryn' – I know you said you want a retail account, so I just wanted to tell you the difference between the retail and wholesale accounts so you can make an informed decision. Wholesale Member: Get the Premium Starter Kit at basically 50% off retail price, everything you need to get you started with essential oils. You can join an exclusive VIP Facebook group just for members (*if you and your team offer this type of group*) to help you learn all about essential oils and how to use them to their fullest potential. I'll also give you a welcome gift to get you started on this journey. PLUS, you'll get 24% off Young Living Essential Oils for life. If you don't make a purchase for 12 months, you'll go inactive, but you can reactivate with no problem. #easypeasy. We have a monthly box option where you earn points. #nopressure

And really quickly, the low down on signing up as Retail Customer - you pay retail prices - 24% over wholesale. You can start out buying individual oils, but there is no kit option. No access to our VIP members group. No gift from me and no savings on your oils. I don't want to be a Debbie Downer about the Retail Account; I just don't see the value in it. However, should you choose to continue with the retail account, I will still be here to assist you in any way I can. I hope that makes sense. Let me know if you have any further questions."

Because I don't recommend being a Retail Customer, I used to think there was no reason to check the Retail Customer report. #wrong #learnedmylesson I've had instances where I've given my link to people who wanted a PSK, but when they went to purchase the kit, they accidentally signed up as a Retail Customer. How did I know this took place? I looked at the Retail Customer report. I would have never realized the error if I hadn't been consistently checking the report. Once I see a person has signed up as a retail customer I do one of two things: 1) I reach out to the customer directly, asking if this is what they meant to do, or 2) I reach out to my business builder who signed them up and let them know they need to reach out to their prospective customer. Here's an easy way you can contact your business builder:

"Hey 'Sally' – I saw Larry might have accidentally signed up as a retail customer. I wanted to remind you that he can't get a

Premium Starter Kit, wholesale pricing, or be part of our Facebook members group as a retail customer. Do you know if that's what he was trying to do? Do you know how to fix that? Let me know if you need any help!! I'm happy to call Leadership if necessary!"

<u>Daily Practice Number 2:</u>
Check your retail customer report.
#boom #easypeasy #lemonsqueezy

Missing Monthly Autoship

Are you guys overwhelmed yet? I understand if you are, but don't worry, you'll get the hang of it. There's so much amazing information that comes from the resources we have at our fingertips. Deep breath. Let's keep going. You just need to be consistent, and you'll get the hang of it.

Another report you can find in your Virtual Office is the *Missing Monthly Autoship* report. This is a great tool that allows you to see who in your downline has missed placing their autoship (Essential Rewards) order in a given month. Once you have that knowledge, you can do something about it. Remember, it's about being leaders; people who provide solutions. Part of being a leader and providing solutions means you cannot live in isolation. Once you know someone has missed the monthly autoship, you've got to do something about it. Contact them to see if the missed autoship was simply a mistake or if they purposely chose not to receive their monthly order. Why is this so crucial to know? Young Living does not offer skip months on Essential Rewards anymore. Let me explain why this is such a big deal. Let's say your member has been on Essential Rewards for 13 months and they are earning 20% of their monthly ER purchase in points. #freeoils If for some reason their Essential Rewards order did not process, their rewards rate will return to what they earn at month 1: 10%. #notokay You will find that people are prone to losing track of their ER order. Whether that's because they're not technologically inclined, are extremely busy, or are just plain disorganized, people may have trouble keeping up with their ER. On top of that, if the person whose ER didn't process is a business person, it is a great teaching opportunity. You can let them know what they'll be missing should they not place their order. It's critical that you know what's going on with your team's monthly autoship so that these things don't fall through the cracks.

If your business builder has been in the game for a while, there's a good chance they may have this under control. However, this isn't always the case. I have met several seasoned business members who didn't realize the importance of monitoring autoship every single day. Remember, don't just assume people know; they may need your help. And, please get this - don't wait for them to ask you for help. They may not even know they need to ask a question, let alone know the right questions to ask. You, as a leader, should always be willing to step out and say,

"I'm stalking your downline and noticed {insert issue}. I'm totally not trying to step on toes, but I wanted to make sure you were aware of what was going on in case you missed it!"

Because I've focused on building relationships, my team is patient with me, even if they've already handled the issue. #teamwork

Daily Practice Number 3:
Check for unprocessed ER orders.

#protip

If a leader wants to manage their own stalking, let them. I'm grateful my upline respects that I take care of my team and do my own stalking and messaging. Nobody wants to be micro-managed. This is where relationships are so crucial; know your people and what they want and need. Even if they want your help stalking, don't message a member without the enroller's permission. Contact the enroller first and let them decide how to handle a situation. Stay in your lane.

Oily Tools

Let's talk about Oily Tools. Let me just get this out of the way - Oily Tools is an amazing resource for your business. It will enhance your ability to know and assist your team as your business grows. #offthechain Now, most of you may have heard of this app, but I know it's possible that some of you haven't. The cool thing about Oily Tools is that there is a free trial as long as you've never used the app before. Just shoot your enroller a message and ask them to gift it to you for a month. But even if you've heard of it, some of you may have resisted the urge to pull the trigger. Or maybe you have the app, but you don't understand what it can do for you. No matter where you are on that spectrum, I want to explain why Oily Tools is such an incredible app for your business.

Understand, I'm speaking as someone who didn't get this tool until I was on the verge of being a Gold team leader, so I am well acquainted with both viewpoints. Here's a caveat, Virtual Office does provide everything you need for your business. However, as you're growing, Oily Tools provides so many extras that only serve to enhance your ability to know and grow your team. I honestly don't know what I'd do without it. The app does cost $6.99 a month, but I believe it is more than worth the investment. Here are just a few reasons why:

Peek at your Paycheck

Yep. This is almost worth the monthly fee by itself. Oily Tools allows you to take a peek at what your paycheck is going to look like each month. Keep in mind; this is just an estimate. What's cool, though, is that throughout the month it shows you more than just the amount of money you'll earn, it provides a breakdown of all the different ways you earn your money. Unilevel, Fast Start, Generations, etc... you name it, they show it.

Another cool way it can be used to help the financial aspect of your business is to look at the amount of money you'd be earning at the next rank. For example, if you're Executive and want to know what your Silver check would look like if you ranked up – you can easily see that with this app. #worthitsweightingold

Money Misser

There is a section in Oily Tools called "Money Misser." It lists those people who are going to miss out on a commission check because their Personal Volume (PV) is below 100 – the amount they need to order on their own account to receive all bonuses and commissions they qualify for. Keep in mind, for those just starting out and selling their first kit; they will get the one time Kit Bonus and Fast Start if they place a 50PV order on their account in the same month.

They will still show up as a Money Missers on Oily Tools because they are losing out on Unilevel Commissions for that month unless they spend 100PV.

This is a brilliant tool for your business, especially if you have a member "accidentally share" like I did and not know they need to place an order to get their Kit Bonus and Fast Start. When I sold a kit, I had ZERO idea that I had to spend 50PV to earn all of the commissions and bonuses. Lucky for me, I had told a friend to log in and order something that was 51.75PV. Psh. I don't believe in luck at all, but you get my drift. It's so easy for someone to miss out on money simply because they don't know what they need in order to qualify for a commission. I also run this report several times towards the end of the month usually because everyone's Essential Rewards order has basically been processed. I'll run it every day about 5 days out and a few times on the last day of the month. Oily Tools helps eliminate people missing out on a paycheck with the money misser report. #dontmissout #moneymoneymoney

Oily Tools Reports
Have you ever tried running any reports from your Virtual Office? There's no better time than the present to begin playing around with that feature. I'm telling you, it will change your business. But, if the

Virtual Office still overwhelms you, you can log into Oily Tools and easily pull up many of the same reports you get in your VO - New Rankers, Executive and above list, Unprocessed ER Orders, and many more. You can even see who is about to rank up by creating a Custom report using OGV parameters. These reports are highly useful. Some you'll use more than others, but they're all there for a reason. You need to be familiar with them and taking advantage of them.

Stats

Stats! What in the world are these all about? Understanding your stats is crucial for gauging the growth of your downline. So, let's take a look at some simple stats that can help change your business.

From Oily Tools, you can see the total members that have ordered this month and the percentage of members who have ordered during the current cycle. But what is even more important is your Essential Rewards percentage. With this awesome stat, you can track your monthly Essential Rewards percentage and look at your growth in this area. A good goal is for you to average about 30% of your team on Essential Rewards. Track this percentage at the end of every month and then do a fun incentive for your team to get that percentage up up UP!

This next stat is one of my absolute favorites; it's Pace OGV and Projected OGV. The Pace OGV gives you the estimated OGV for the end of the month as a trended calculation, while your projected OGV gives you the estimated OGV for the end of the month using your current OGV and outstanding ER orders. #brilliant #gamechanger

There are tons of other stats specifically regarding your team's Essential Rewards orders processing, average ER order, total enrollments, percentages at each rank and MORE. Like I said, I believe that this app is a steal at $6.99 a month. It has the potential to completely revolutionize your business. I would encourage you to jump on board as soon as you can.

Daily Practice Number 4:
Check Oily Tools reports.

Monthly Promotions

Are you concerned about people missing out on the monthly promos? There's a surefire way to make sure your people are getting all they can get. All you need to do, if they are on ER, is look at their forecast PV by hovering your mouse cursor over the ER box in the *Autoship* column of *My Organization* in the VO. So many times, I've seen an order that has fallen short of that month's promotion levels. I hate it when people miss out on freebies! So, what do I do? I let them know. I reach out to those whose orders are set to be close to a promotional level and inform them of how much they need to add to their order to receive that month's promotional product. #FreeStuff. Many times, the person is just shy of the purchase amount needed to qualify, so they only need to add a small amount. For orders that have already processed, this is a great time to let them know that they don't want to miss out on the promos next month.

#protip

If you aren't in the habit of regularly checking the monthly promotions, you may not know what to do. Start by looking for a trend in a given member's orders. Is there a pattern to what they're ordering? Look to see if their orders have been close to the 100/190/250/300PV promotional tiers. Young Living typically offers their monthly promos for orders reaching these levels. They give away certain oils and products each month to those ordering a particular PV amount *in a single order* (not cumulative orders throughout the month). We want to make sure everyone is aware of the freebies that are available to them.
#everyonelovesfree #freeisbest

PV Assistant

PV Assistant is kind of a huge deal. It doesn't get as much attention as it should, so I want to make sure you understand what it is. You know that moment where your Essential Rewards processes and one of the items on your order goes out of stock? That moment of terror where you have gone below your desired PV amount and will miss out on free products or worse, commissions? Fear no more. PV Assistant has got you and your downline's backs. Everyone on ER should be signed up for this baby.

So what is PV Assistant exactly? PV Assistant allows you to create a monthly PV goal, starting at 50pv. You can change it monthly to ensure you hit your desired monthly PV Promotions: 100, 190, 250, 300...etc. The first item on your list gets pulled first. If your Essential Rewards order falls below your customizable PV goal, the assistant will automatically add an item(s) from your wish list so that you always meet your goal. #gotyourback

To sign up for PV Assistant, go to your Virtual Office and click on *Essential Rewards*, then *PV Assistant*. Set the PV level that you want to be sure to hit, choose your favorite products that you never want to be without, and you're all set!!

You can check to see if your ER members are enrolled in the PV Assistant by looking at *My*

Organization on your VO and looking next to the ER Box in the *Autoship* column. If they are enrolled in the PV Assistant, you will see a white checkmark in a green shield next to it. If you don't see that, I HIGHLY recommend you reach out to them and tell them about it!

Daily Practice Number 5:
Check your members' pending PV and PV Assistant

OGV Tracking

Organization Growth Volume is something that each person needs to be tracking every single day. This is something my sponsor pushed on me big time. There are no ifs, ands, or buts about it. DO IT! Now, I'm going to be real with you, one of my problems is that I assume daily OGV tracking is a habit that EVERYONE is currently practicing. Time and time again I'm confronted with the fact that this assumption couldn't be further from the truth. I'm amazed when I speak at events to hear that on average, 90% of the people I speak with do not utilize this simple way of stalking their downline. I cannot stress this enough: track your OGV daily, no matter your current rank. I don't care if you think, "my OGV is too small to track." DO IT ANYWAY! Write down your OGV and the number of members in your downline, and do it EVERY. SINGLE. DAY. EVEN IF THE NUMBERS ONLY CHANGE A FEW TIMES IN A MONTH.

Okay sorry, I get a little heated about that. When you track your downline (through your OGV, member count, and even your leg leaders' OGV), you are getting to know how your team works just a little bit more. It's really amazing to see the difference when you look back at different days and years. I honestly feel like this is one of the most important things you can do for your business. When I get discouraged, I find encouragement when I look at my last 2 years of growth and can see how far we've come. Start the habit NOW! #notyelling #wellmaybejustalittle

---

#protip

We've got to document our journey. That's what OGV tracking is all about. Pick a daily time that works for you. Start today! Next, write down the OGV for each of your Leg Leaders. This will allow you to keep track of your own growth, as well as the growth in each of your legs in the days and months ahead. It may seem inconsequential at first but, as you're able to track where you've been, you will see the benefits of this indispensable step.

#protip

A part of **OGV** tracking is keeping tabs on your team's kit sales. Write down the number of your team's new kit sales every day. For me, this works best by jotting them down on a calendar or on a single piece of paper. If you're a visual learner like me, it really helps to see it all laid out in one place. Why do I do this? I can actually track which day of the week my team sells the most kits. **HOW COOL IS THAT?** #prettycool This helps me to see how we are doing every month and if I need to do an incentive or special to help support my team. It also helps me track my biggest days during the month and allows me to track OGV spikes if a special product comes back in stock. When Peace and Calming or Valor comes back in, I write down my **OGV** and then put an asterisk next to it and say, "Valor back in stock." This is so I can track to see how much our team grew just from that one oil coming back. At the end of the day, it doesn't matter **HOW** you're writing it down, just make sure that you **ARE** writing it down.

Your Mind is not a Steel Trap

"The biggest lie I tell myself is:
I don't need to write that down; I'll remember it."
~Anonymous

I absolutely love this quote because it's SO true. I'm the opposite of an elephant. I remember nothing. I will say I'm pretty good with remembering people, just not details. So, this part of the process is easier for me than some because I know that if I don't write things down, I have no hope of remembering much at all. You may have an amazing mind, but you've got to understand something; you won't remember where you've been unless you write it down. And, if you don't know where you've been, how can you know how far you've come? And if you don't know how far you've come, how do you know where to go from here? See how this all adds up? OGV tracking is vital to growing your business and knowing where you're going. It will enable you to understand when it's time to think through adjustments, as well as celebrate the victories that have come along the way.

#example

Without tracking my OGV, I never would have known that in the middle of June 2014 my team was at 10,951.50 OGV and by the middle of June 2015, it had grown to 66,453.20! #hugedeal #writeitdown Talk about excited, pumped, ecstatic! Whatever word you want to use, that was me. How do I know what my OGV was on June 15 of both 2014 and 2015? I tracked my OGV; I wrote it down. By practicing this little step, I knew where I had been. As a result, I could see how far I had come, and I knew I was on the right path going ahead. This was a cause for celebration. We all like parties, right? How can you throw a party if you don't know you should be celebrating? It's that simple.

STOP!

I want you to do something before you read any further. Grab that pen and paper I told you to have on standby. Open up your Virtual Office and do exactly what I just told you to do; write down your OGV, the OGV of your leg leaders, and the number of members in your organization. Do it. RIGHT NOW! I'm waiting. #notsobad #youllthankmelater

Daily practice number 6:
Track your team's OGV and Kit Sales.

New Members

Next up we have the "New Members" tab in the Virtual Office. It's good to get into the habit of checking the sponsor and enroller when you notice new people in your downline. If the sponsor and enroller are the same, you know they haven't been restructured (strategically placed). The enroller may be leaving them on their level 1 because of their potential to become a business builder. However, there is a possibility that the enroller may have forgotten to restructure them after they enrolled. It helps your downline if you are keeping tabs on the new members, so your business builders don't miss the short window to get this done easily.

I try to give my people a little time to decide where they're going to place their new members before contacting them. Again, you want to be careful not to micro-manage. But as long as you're being kind and genuine, most people appreciate a reminder. Young Living gives you several days after a member enrolls to restructure. Call Member Services or hop on Live Chat and you can get everything squared away. I highly recommend you restructure within the initially allotted time frame because after that period of time you must then email resolutions@youngliving.com and wait for them to make the change. Get with your upline to find out the specifics like the amount of time you have to restructure and the wording you should use while doing so. I always try to remind my business builders about restructuring as often as possible because those days go by QUICKLY. #signupallthepeople #oilsineveryhome

Daily practice number 7:
Check for New Members.

For Silvers & Above - New Member Placements

I wanted to take a minute to share something with those of you who are at the rank of Silver or above. I can remember a few times, at the beginning of this journey, checking my downline and thinking, "Oh look, my member count just jumped." After stalking my downline, I came to a name that I didn't recognize. What I learned was that Young Living has a placement program.

Here's what you need to know: When checking your downline, look for any new members that may have been placed there via Young Living's placement program. If you are an active Silver leader, Young Living will place people from your area in your downline. Yes, this is an actual thing, and it's amazing! What is the placement program all about? While you and I may live in a world where it's hard to imagine someone not knowing about YLEO, there are millions of people who haven't. But when someone hears about Young Living and signs up without a sponsor, they are like orphans. So, Young Living looks for people - active Silver leaders or above - to care for these "orphans." It doesn't always result in much for your business, but sometimes it does. Currently, I have several placements who are on ER, and one of my "orphans" is even doing the business! You just never know who you might get. Once someone has been placed in your organization, you will need to reach out to them and restructure them, should you choose, within the allotted timeframe. If you aren't stalking your downline daily, you may miss that initial window.

#protip

If the placement is a retail customer, and they choose to stay that way after you contact them, I would suggest leaving them on your level one. If you were to restructure a retail customer off your level one, you would not receive full commission on them. You only receive full commission on level one retail customers.

Here is a sample e-mail that you can send to any "orphans" that Young Living has placed in your organization:

"Good Morning and happy Friday! I hope you are enjoying some sunshine and have fun plans this weekend! Young Living has connected us so I can help you in this oily journey! I wanted to let you know that I can add you to our Facebook group that provides classes and a community that can help you with oily tips! If you'd like to share your oils with friends, we also have a group to help you with that.

I also wanted to point out that every month Young Living provides monthly promos. I would be happy to tell you about the promos every month if you'd like. I hope you know that I am ALWAYS available to answer questions and help you get the most out of your oils! Since I do the "business" end of Young Living, I can be a liaison between you and YL if there are any issues with orders, questions about promos, etc.

Thanks for trusting me to be your oil lady. I love getting to do this every day, and I am thankful for the opportunity to support you in this journey! Again, please reach out if you need any help with your oils!!"

It really is that simple. I'll usually put my contact information and website so people can easily contact me should they so choose. #getit #silverandabove #booyah

Chapter 6: Weekly Whisperings

Let's move on to the things you should be doing on a weekly basis to know and grow your team. These are practices you don't necessarily need to stay on top of daily but should be doing weekly to keep your organization organized.

Personally Enrolled Wholesale Members

Every single week, once a week, I check on my personally enrolled. This entails more than just looking at their names on a screen; I am actively involved with them. Understand, to me, it doesn't matter whether they're a wholesale member or a business builder, I watch their accounts. #itsaboutpeople Again, I know I've said it over and over, but I want you to get it; I want to create a family atmosphere. How can I do that if I don't know what's going on? So, I stalk all my personally enrolled, no matter who they are. I want them to know I care about them. I want them to know that they're all important to me.

Let's talk specifically about wholesale members. These people are important to me and to my business. I want to make sure my wholesale members have been consistently using their oils. They made a big purchase, and I want them to get the most out of their investment. The oils are not a waste of money, so I don't want anyone to feel like they wasted their money just because they are not using the product. This is where relationships are key: focus on the person and help them get the most out of their investment!!

After they're comfortable using the oils in their kit, it's our job to check to see if they need any help ordering additional products or reordering their favorites. #hello #essentialrewards If they haven't set up ER, but are ready to reorder, reach out and share with them the benefits of that program. Regardless, always drop in to see if they are loving their oils and if they need any additional help. Everyone is different; some people may want a phone call or text. Others may want an email. Find out what matters to your personally enrolled in terms of communication, and be available to them.

#example
One of my personally enrolled had a unique way of communicating. They wanted to use the app "Voxer" - an app that functions as sort of a walkie talkie. So what did I do? I downloaded it and used it just for her. This allowed me to meet her needs specifically and connect with her. It meant a lot to her that I

would use what worked best for her and she immediately felt more comfortable and connected.

<u>Weekly Practice Number 1</u>:
Reach out to your personally enrolled wholesale members.

Business Builders

Here's the process I go through for my Business Builders. The first thing I check is to make sure they have placed at least a 50 OR 100 PV order. Why the difference in PV? I need to know which one is best for the person. Some people are just doing the business casually. If this is the case, they only need a 50 PV order to get the Kit Bonus and Fast Start. Others are trying to make this their main source of income. These business builders need to place an order of at least 100 PV to get all of the bonuses and commissions available to them.

Let me say something about the casual business builder (those that sell a kit here and there but aren't doing the business full-time). I have heard some people allude to the fact that it's a waste of time to invest in people who are doing the business "accidentally," but I totally disagree. After all, that's exactly what I was in the beginning. I believe that both types of kit sellers are important to your business, that's why I check all of my business builders to make sure that they do not have any personally enrolled people that they need to restructure. I check to make sure that they have viable business legs and that they are setting them up correctly. I want everyone to be successful, and by me stalking my downline, I can give them every opportunity to be just that.

Weekly Practice Number 2:
Reach out to your business builders.

#protip

You might be thinking, "Why in the world does she think it's worth her time to invest in both types of business builders?" Everyone is at a different stage of life. Some are ready, chomping at the bit to get this party started. Others may not be ready to go all in, they may just share casually. That's perfectly fine. In fact, I have several Executives, Silvers and even a Gold who went the way of the casual business builder. When they first started, they weren't ready to dive in. However, I was patient, and nurtured that relationship knowing where they were. Eventually, they saw the potential, and now they're gangbusters. #ballstothewalls

---

#protip

I always encourage my business builders to provide educational opportunities for their new members. What I've learned is that these opportunities seem to go over best with my downline when I'm not the only one teaching them. When educational opportunities come from other leaders, especially those with whom the new member has a relationship, it's very beneficial. People want to hear from their friends.

#protip

Educational classes should be more than just a one-time thing; they should be done on a regular basis. Hosting a 102 Class (for after the initial kit oils) and an Essential Rewards class on a monthly or bi-monthly basis is super important to help your people get the most out of their memberships and products. #knowledgeispower #educateyourmembers

Messaging within the Virtual Office

This is something that has significantly improved the efficiency of my business and keeping in contact with my team on a weekly basis. I love this feature in the Virtual Office. What's so cool about this tool? You can use this system to message the people in your downline in various ways. For instance, you can send a message to those who bought their kit directly from you. If you have something that you want to communicate to your entire team you can do that as well. Or you can send out a note to specific pockets of your team. Let's learn more about this.

Messaging your entire team
Go to *My Organization*, *Reports*, click on *All Accounts*. In the right-hand corner, there's a link that says: "Send Message to Report." This will send a message to every account in your downline. This is a great way to do team incentives. However, I would recommend checking with your business leaders before you do this. It can get messy really fast if your downline doesn't want contact or if your business leaders already have a plan of their own. Remember that a huge part of being a leader is respecting your members' wishes. There's a huge potential for trust to go right out the door if you contact a business builder's team member without talking to them first. #berespectful Once everyone is on board, send out

that incentive using the "Send Message to Report" link.

Messaging PERSONAL kit sales only

Go to *My Organization*, *Reports*, click on *Personally Enrolled*. In the right-hand corner, there's a link that says: "Send message to report." This will send a message only to those whom you've personally enrolled. This is great when your team has gotten big, and you'd like to do something special for just your personally enrolled. I love to connect with them as much as possible. In reality, I use three methods to stay connected with my personally enrolled: the Virtual Office, texting, or Facebook Messenger. #justconnect

Messaging Specific Reports

Let's chat about some of the specific reports that you can pull, then see how and why you might use them. Start out by going to *My Organization*, *Reports*, and clicking on *All Accounts*. At this point, you can *Customize* by choosing a number of different options.

For our purposes, let's use "Personally Enrolled By." Click on *Member ID* and then type in the member number of the enroller you want shown. In the right-hand corner, you'll again see the link that says, "Send message to report." This allows you to message only people personally enrolled by one of your business builders. Again, I would only do this with permission from your business builder. When might you use this function? If you're brainstorming with your business builder and want to offer something fun to their personally enrolled, this would be the time to utilize this feature.

There are quite a few reports you can run in a similar manner. For instance, you can pick out members in specific states if you're doing a class in the area and want to invite them. You can message members who aren't on Essential Rewards if you're doing an incentive if they enroll. Or you can pull up a report to message those who don't have PV assistant, reminding them that this feature will keep them from falling below their desired PV. The list goes on and on. #somanyoptions #timetoexplore

Messaging Without Your Mermaid Leg
Now, let's say EVENTUALLY you have what people refer to as a "Mermaid Leg." A Mermaid Leg is usually referring to a group within your downline, that has grown so large that it has the ability, should they choose, to branch out and start their own Facebook group (for business, members, or both). This leg may want you involved, or they may want to be completely autonomous. Either way, it's totally up to them. #reproducingreproducers So, let's say you want to

message your entire downline, but you don't want anyone in the Mermaid Leg to receive the email. YOU CAN DO THAT! Yep. #forreal All you do is you go to *My Organization*, *Reports*, click on *All Accounts*, click on *Customize*, go down and pick *Not Within the Organization of*, then click *Member ID* and type in your KICK BUTT (don't actually type this) Mermaid Leg leader's member number, then click *Apply*. Voila! You've created a message to go to everyone except that specific leg. If you have more than one leg you want to be excluded, simply click *Add*, repeat the process and add another leg. Then "Send Message to Report"!! All set! That message will go to everyone except those on the excluded list.

Message Specific Legs

In the same way, you can message SPECIFIC legs that are anywhere in your downline through the Virtual Office, while leaving other legs off.

Let's say you want to offer an incentive to help grow your third leg so you can hit Gold. Well, if your first two legs already qualify you for Gold at 6,000 OGV each, there's no reason to message them for this push. So, you want to create a special message just for that third leg. You do that by going to the Reports section of your VO, clicking on *All Accounts*, *Customize*, *Within the Organization of*, *Member ID*, then type the member number of the person who's at the top of that leg. Once again, you're all set. You can now send that specific leg a message (with your leg leader's approval) without including anyone else! #pathtogold

Other Messaging Tips

Some people get great response emailing within the Virtual Office, and others see none at all. This is something you will need to play around with to find out what works for you and your team. If messaging through the Virtual Office doesn't work, consider a texting program. This provides a fun way give some oily education while texting, I mean who doesn't text? #thisis2017 Consider doing whatever works for your members. Remember how I downloaded Voxer for one of my members? Be willing to do what you can to connect with your people.

I'm telling you all this so that you will know how to better utilize your Virtual Office to keep in contact with your downline. There are a ton of things you can do in there, and it's fun to use more tools as your downline grows. You may not need all of these immediately, BUT you will use them down the road!!

<u>Weekly Practice Number 3</u>:
Reach out to your downline using whichever method works best for your team; within the VO or utilizing other platforms.

#protip

VO messages go to the member's email address on file. It's important to know they can unsubscribe from these, so make sure you aren't spamming them with emails every day. #annoying #byebyebye #blocked Keep the communication consistent, but spaced out. Stick to the important things.

#protip

It doesn't always have to be about oils or this business. It's really easy to get caught up in a bad habit of only communicating business stuff. It's even more difficult to get out of the habit. I try to be consistent in talking to my team about life as well. Stay in touch through Facebook. Oddly enough, I feel SUPER loved when I see my sponsor commenting on my posts. It matters that she takes the time to care about what is going on in my life and what's really important to me. Maybe you can put that on your list of things to do: comment on your team's posts regularly. #beauthentic #trulycare

Chapter 7: Monthly Whisperings

The last step of Downline Whispering are those things should be done on a monthly basis. These steps are vital, but they don't need to be done on a daily or even weekly basis. They are the things we should be doing each month to help know and grow our teams.

Team Whisperings

The definition of training is "The action of teaching a person a particular skill or type of behavior." You want to make sure you're doing the work to SHOW your people how to do things themselves, otherwise, you're going to end up stretching yourself thin. To do this, every month I work hard to provide the training that my team needs to grow. I do several different things depending on the person/people I'm trying to reach:

- Offer a Facetime/phone call date to answer questions
- Look through their downline with them
- Strategically help them to build their business legs
- Have a business class for business members
- Do a training series in the business group

- Host online classes and let them add their people
- Provide incentives or team activities with the purpose to grow us closer together and learn about each other
- Help foster groups for each business leg, so they all know each other and benefit from each other's experiences and support
- Travel and do classes for team members

<u>**Monthly practice number 1:**</u>
Connect with your team in multiple ways.

Mentoring

I believe that mentoring is a crucial component of not just building a successful business, but also creating a family atmosphere. Why? Mentoring is all about relationships. Jake always tells a story of when he was in college. One day, after a basketball practice, his coach asked the team, "how do you spell love?" All of the guys assumed it was some type of trick question, but they didn't know exactly how. Eventually, after everyone was finished looking around at each other dumbfounded, one of the guys bit, "L.O.V.E?" The coach said, "No. You spell it T.I.M.E." The point he was trying to make is that you don't really love someone if you're not willing to put the time investment into that person. If I say I love someone, they will know it's true by the time I spend with them. The same is true in this business. If I want to create a family atmosphere and build a successful team, I must put in the time. So, I want to share with you some of the ways I go about doing this.

One thing that is super important is for my team to know that I am available for them; it lets them know that they are a priority of mine. Be available, but not TOO available. You don't want people wondering where you went, but you also want people to know that you're not on call 24/7. After all, how can I truly mentor someone if I'm never available or if I'm burned out from not setting boundaries?

But it's about more than just being available; it's also about being transparent. I often ask the people in my team if they are getting what they need from me as a leader. Listen, you can't force desire. Trying to make someone do this biz or work as hard as you work or care as much as you care is only going to push them away. All you can really do is try to inspire them. You do this by doing everything you can to provide them with everything they need to be successful. It's all about time. But don't forget, success is different for everyone. It would probably be very beneficial for you to ask the business builders on your team, "how do you define success?" This will enable you to better customize your efforts to meet their needs.

But what about the nitty gritty? What do I do if I'm available and transparent and someone takes me up on the offer to mentor them? Starting off, here are questions I ask new people who want mentoring.

What are your business goals? Do you have short term (1-3 months), annual, and long term (3-5 year) goals? Can I help you work through those by using the SMART system?

SMART goals are defined on MindTools.com as:

Specific: What do you want to accomplish? Who is involved? Where is it located?

Measurable: How much? How many? How will I know when it is accomplished?

Achievable: How realistic is this goal? How can I accomplish this goal?

Relevant: Is this the right time? Does this match our needs? Does this seem worthwhile?

Time Bound: What can I do today? What can I do this month? When do I want this accomplished?

~ Do you have a "WHY"? This is the main reason you're doing this business. What drives you to keep going even when you want to throw in the towel. Think about your dreams and what is so important to you to achieve that it keeps you going in the slumps.

~ What are your strengths? If you don't really know, I suggest Strengthfinders 2.0. We focus on strengths over weaknesses.

~ What are some specific ways you see me supporting you in this business?

~ What is the best way for us to communicate? What's your preferred way of communication?

~ How would you like to grow your business? (In person classes, social media...etc.)

If they want to utilize social media to grow their business, I'll ask:

~ Are you willing to have an open discussion about social media and how to structure your use of it to benefit your business?

~ How do you think you do on social media?

~ What are some things that you could do better in regards to your social media usage?

~ Can I look at your social media and then schedule another call so I can share with you some tips and we can work on it together?

These questions allow me to tailor how I help each person, dependent on their goals and strengths. After we have moved through this "introductory" period, I then move on to more intensive questions geared toward people who want a 45-day mentoring program. It's really important that you take intense notes when you're meeting with your business builders. Remember what I said about the biggest lie you tell yourself? You won't remember in a year, so write it down and update as your team's goals and "why's" change.

One of my favorite reports to run in the VO for my business builders is when they say they want to grow their OGV, but say they just can't. I go to *Reports*, *Within Organization of*, then *Customize* by clicking *Member ID* and type in their member number. Then I *Customize* with *0 PV* and hit *Apply*. This report shows you everyone in their organization that hasn't ordered that month. If it's the beginning of the month or mid-way through, I will usually have them run this report for the month prior so that they can see the fullness of the report. This allows them to focus on the people who did not order the prior month and devote more time to them. Have they cracked open their kit? Do they know how to use their oils to the fullest? Do they know how to reorder and about ER? Could they benefit in sharing with others so they can get their oils paid for and order monthly? If it isn't their personally enrolled member, I will again recommend that the business builder reach out to that person's enroller first, rather than contacting another business builder's member.

Worst case, you ask these "0's" if you can help them and they tell you "nope." Then you write down their name and don't contact them anymore. The thing is, you won't know if you don't ask them. #dontbescared

One last thing about mentoring. I said earlier; you can't make anyone want this as much as you do. However, I've learned that your believing in something goes a long way toward your team believing. If you don't believe in the product and the business model that has been provided, well then, it's likely your people will struggle with this as well. When you believe in it, and that belief is evident to everyone around you, it's contagious. That's the starting point of inspiration. #believe

<u>Monthly Practice Number 2:</u>
Pour into your team and see what
each individual needs.

Inactive Members

If you've been doing this business for a year or longer, you may have some people in your downline who are on the verge of going inactive (those who have not ordered in the past 12 months). Young Living recently upgraded the Virtual Office and made it SO EASY for us to track the members who are about to go inactive. On the summary page in your VO, go to the bottom right-hand corner and click *About to Go Inactive*. This will show you the people that have not ordered in the past year and whose accounts are about to become inactive. Look at this report every month so you can reach out and let those people know where they stand. #snatchthembackup

Here's a sample of a message I have sent to potential inactive members. I tweak this based on the relationship I have with the person I'm contacting!

Hey _____, Hope all is well with you and your fam! I saw you guys just got a new dog! How fun! Is {insert child} just so in love?!?!

Just wanted to give you a quick heads up that your Young Living account is about to go inactive. Your last order was placed on XX/XX/20XX and after a year of no activity, accounts are deactivated. If you would like to keep your wholesale membership, which allows you to purchase products for 24% off retail, simply place a 50pv order before XX/XX. To place an order, login here with your member number (which is XXXXX) and your password. www.youngliving.com/vo I do hope you're loving your oils, but of course, there is never any pressure to reorder. Just wanted to let you know about your account status. And as always, if you need help knowing how to use the oils you have or deciding which oils to add to your arsenal, please let me know. I'm here to help you! Have a great week - hope to chat with you soon!

Monthly Practice Number 3:
Check for members about to go inactive and contact them.

#protip

A monthly newsletter is a great way to keep up communication with your people. It also utilizes what we learned in the previous chapter: messaging your personally enrolled members through the Virtual Office Message System. The only bummer is that the Virtual Office does not currently allow for any graphics to be added to the message. If you'd like to add graphics to your newsletter, Mail Chimp is a great resource to use.

PGV – Personal Growth Volume

To qualify for any rank Silver or above, you need 1,000 PGV. Are you ready? Stay with me for this. It can be super confusing, so I'm going to give you Young Living's description and then try to clarify it later. According to Young Living:

Personal Group Volume is determined by the sales volume of the organization directly supported by the distributor. PGV accumulates throughout each commission period. This is the sum of PV from the distributor down to, but not including, the next Silver or higher rank for each leg of the sales organization. PGV in these cases does not include any Silver or higher rank and the entirety of volume in their organization. PGV also does not include any volume from qualifying legs used for rank qualification in a commission period.

Understanding PGV is probably one of the most confusing things for people to grasp. The easiest way for me to break this down is to say that PGV is all of your PV and OGV that is outside of your qualifying legs for Silver or higher. So, if you're a Gold, your first 3 legs of 6,000 or higher do not count towards your PGV. Your PGV is your PV (your personal order) PLUS any orders outside of your qualifying legs. This is absolutely something you must triple check for your people. I've seen some big mistakes happen because PGV wasn't counted accurately. Even though I'm pretty experienced with PGV now, I still find myself calling Leadership "just to make sure." Better safe than sorry. #ainttooproudtocheck

<u>**Monthly practice number 4:**</u>
Start learning about PGV or watch it like a hawk.

End of the Month Whispering

As I'm sure you're well aware, the end of every month is wild. This is when I stalk my downline like a crazy person. Here are some of my must do's when it comes to end of the month Downline Whispering:

● Contact anyone who is about to miss out on money because they haven't placed the necessary order. Money Misser on Oily Tools helps with this. I do this for everyone in my team, but I reach out to my Silvers and above (sometimes Executives, depending on the dynamic) if they are not my personally enrolled. This allows me to look out for my team but not step on toes or have multiple people message the a member. I want my team not to need me, but everyone needs a reminder here and there.

● If someone is close to a rank, message them and help them formulate a plan so they can achieve it.

● Contact any prospects who haven't completed their sign up process (*Prospects* tab in your VO).

● When scrolling through your VO, it will be easy to see those members who have been purchasing BUT ARE NOT ON ER #sayitaintso. You can run a report for this very easily. Go to *Reports*, click on *Members,* then go all the way down the list to *Essential Rewards Status,* click *is* and then choose *No ER* from the drop down options. Reach out to the enroller to see if they have had an opportunity to talk to them about ER. You could even help the leader hold an ER class for those unfamiliar with ER or its benefits.

<u>Monthly practice number 5:</u>
Look out for your team with
end of month stalking.

#protip

This one comes from my friend, Rosy – yes, the same Rosy that gave me my creepy stalker name: "I set aside several pages in a folder to keep track of my downline and write down all of the people who have hit rank. I have a page for each rank with a list of names. I specifically write down the month and year that someone hit Executive so I can be mindful of Silver in 6. {Silver in 6 (Si6) is when you hit Silver within 6 months of hitting the rank of Executive. You get gifts from YL when you make it!} This practice will also be helpful to help you recognize if someone is falling back or maintaining rank."

Chapter 8: Random Virtual Office Whispering

How are you doing? Are you feeling great about Whispering to your Downline, or are you feeling stressed out? Running reports isn't all fun and games, but it's really beneficial to your business. I haven't even hit on half of the reports, so please know that there are for sure TONS of other reports that you can run in your Virtual Office. I want to quickly talk to you about some of my favorites.

By going directly to *My Organization* in the Virtual Office, there are 17 reports that you can easily run without even a second thought. There's really no reason why you shouldn't be running these monthly (or more often) for your business. Here's a brief rundown of these reports.

All Accounts – Your entire downline with all of your legs in place.

Members (Distributors) – Your entire downline automatically in order from highest OGV to lowest OGV. You're also able to click on the column titles, for instance, "Level," and it will put your downline in order of your level 1 down to the lowest level underneath you. Click it again, and it will start with your lowest level up to your highest level. You can also sort according to their name in alphabetical order, high or low PV, and even by their ER date!

Leaders – Your Silver or above team leaders. It really comes in handy when you are at the end of the month and referring back to the previous month to see who still needs to rank up to maintain Silver or above ranks and might need a hand.

Retail Customers – This is a great way to track all of your retail customers to see if they need help placing an order or if they'd like a Premium Starter Kit instead. Some people just need to be asked. Don't let fear control you. The worst thing they can say is no.

Accounts with Autoship – How amazing is this report? You can see how many people are already on autoship with this feature!

Accounts without Autoship – This really helps you gauge your members who are ordering without Essential Rewards. Sometimes people just don't want to be on ER but again, the worst case scenario is you tell them about its benefits, and they say no.

Accounts with Email – When sending messages through your VO, this is who is getting those messages.

Accounts without Email – These are the people that you're not able to reach through the messaging feature in your VO.

Personally Enrolled – This gives you all of your personally enrolled listed in one place. I use this list when I'm sending happy mail.

On Hold – anyone who has some type of issue with their account or hasn't completed a part of the signup process will have a red triangle with an exclamation mark in the middle. Contact Member Services on their behalf to see what's going on.

Zero PV – I LOVE running this report at the end of the month so I can see how many on my team didn't order. I really encourage my team to reach out to those people to see if they are not understanding the oily lifestyle.

Missing Current Month Autoship – BRILLIANT. Run this report at the end of the month so you can see who may have accidentally skipped their ER and will have to go all the way back to the beginning percentage. #nooooooo

Last Order Date – You want to see when everyone in your downline ordered last? Click on this report.

Rank Advancement – This is also one of my absolute favorites. This report shows you a member's highest paid rank, their previous month's rank, and their current month's rank. I LOVE it so much. Makes it so much easier to track.

Forecast PV – This report can help you catch the people who may have 189PV scheduled on their ER and just need 1PV to get the 190PV promos added. Check this report throughout the month.

You can also *CUSTOMIZE* all these reports to make up your own – which is where I taught you about "within the organization of..."

In addition to all of this, Young Living is constantly making upgrades to the Virtual Office! They are always trying to improve their business tools to give us every opportunity to make our business as successful as possible. Once you're familiar with the basics of the VO, anything else that's added should be fairly easy to learn. There are so many great things at your fingertips in the Virtual Office; you just need to take the time to look around and explore!

Chapter 9: Education Through Social Media

I know this doesn't have anything to do with your Virtual Office, but being actively involved in your team's oily education group on Facebook, or any other social media platform, will return huge dividends. More than likely, you won't always see immediate results, but the outcome will be well worth the effort. Education is really what I want to emphasize here. #oilyeducators Educational opportunities can make or break your business; it all boils down to you and your involvement. Personally, I have used Facebook to not only expand my reach and grow my business but also to help manage my organization. If used properly, it can be an incredible tool to not only support business members but also provide you with the opportunity to educate members and non-members alike.

I'm not suggesting you go out and immediately start your own Facebook group. #nope #nonono If your upline already has an educational group for their team, take advantage of the infrastructure they have built! They've implemented these groups to educate their downline – you and your members. Use these groups to devour all the information you can and share your experiences and knowledge with others.

113

Another reason you need to be involved? Presence. Being present in these groups speaks volumes to the members on your team. It lets your people know how serious you are about your oils and your business. The bigger your presence, the more "love" you're displaying. #timespellslove

---

#protip

Why is being present in your Facebook groups is so crucial? Facebook has some pretty wild algorithms that will help you with your Facebook presence. The more interactive you are, the bigger your Facebook footprint and the more you're showing your people how much you really care about them, the oils and your business. When you post and comment in groups, the people you added have a higher chance of seeing your interactions. This encourages them to get involved in the group. The more involved they are in the group, the more likely they are to use their products. This is beneficial in any type of group. The more active you are, the more you'll encourage your people to be active.

To Stay or Leave

I mentioned not starting your own Facebook group right away. In the beginning, it is definitely better to take advantage of the education and experience in an established group. But I've dealt with an issue that eventually may arise for you; whether you should stay in your upline's group, or leave to start your own. There are a few reasons I suggest staying in your upline's group for as long as possible.

1) Beginning and effectively running your own Facebook group takes A LOT of time, effort, and hard work. On top of that, once you've started the group, "it" never really ends. You don't get a break from running the group. It's all on you. #itcanbeexhausting Why do you need to know this? Many people aren't ready to put in the time and effort to start and effectively run a Facebook group. Sure, you might be able to start a group, but we want to be excellent in what we do. To start and manage a group the way it should be requires a lot. Most people don't understand the cost before they begin the process.

2) People want to be involved in a group that is active. People like to be where the action is; action normally breeds excitement. Smaller groups tend to have "crickets," leading to inactivity. That can be super discouraging for you and your members. Why add that stress to your life if you don't need to?

3) "If it ain't broke...," I think you know the rest. I've seen people who've broken off to start their own groups way too soon, with disastrous results. If your upline has a group and everything is kosher, use it!! Most uplines in this business want you to succeed, and the group is there to provide you with even more resources to help you and your team to be successful. #dontbeprideful

Don't Stow and Go

As you're using your team's groups, understand this: the groups are not there for you to simply drop a member in, only to have you run and disappear. Running a group, no matter its purpose, takes a lot of time and energy. Be respectful. Your leader has put a lot into making these groups beneficial for everyone involved. Not to mention, the member you added to the group is your responsibility, per Young Living's Policies and Procedures. You can't expect them to think they're like family to you, let alone grow a business, if you're pawning them off on other people. Don't be one of those "stow and go" people where you add a member to a group, then disappear. #dontstowandgo As I said earlier, you need to be actively involved. Ask questions. Answer questions. Interact with the other members. Other leaders are in there supporting your team by engaging and answering questions. Keep the excitement going, support others on your team, and let your members see you participating.

#protip

If you want more responsibility within the group, ask the leader how you can help them. Then actually follow through and do the job. #dontbackout #thatbreakstrust This is a great way to not only be present, but also help your leader with running the group. Taking on a heavier load in your leader's group is also a good way to give you a taste of what it's like to run your own group. #preparingyoutolead

---

Thanksgiving Dinner

Being present on social media doesn't have to be something that's difficult or elaborate. I don't know if you had the blessing of being a part of a solid family growing up, but I did. If you didn't, I am so sorry. I hope at some point you can experience the beauty of what family really is. One of the things I remember vividly about our family was our times around the Thanksgiving dinner table. All the stories that were shared, tears that were shed, and laughs that were had will stick with me for the rest of my life. As I think back on those times, I can remember that the stories varied greatly; we didn't just talk about one topic. We shared life as a family. We talked about what was happening in our lives. That's how I want you to think about your groups. We want this business to be more than just a business; we want it to be a family. If you view the people in your groups as an extension of your family, the groups can have an environment much like the Thanksgiving dinner table; a place where everyone can share their stories.

I use social media to share my story. Through my story, I'm able to let others know how this company has changed my life. At the same time, these groups allow me the opportunity to share with the world that I am more than just a Young Living business builder. I'm letting them into my life on a personal level. I'm inviting them into my family.

Think About It

How can you become better at expanding your presence on social media? Ask yourself a few things as you think through this topic:

- Are you actively involved on Facebook and other social media platforms?
- Does your upline have a Facebook group?
- Are you a part of that group?

- How could you become more involved?
- Is the group a tight knit community?
- Why or why not?
- How could you help facilitate a family atmosphere?
- What responsibilities could you ask to take over?

#protip

There's something that seems to be sorely missing in our world today - Facebook etiquette. While Facebook can be a great resource, most of us have experienced some pretty frustrating things – like the time that person messaged you. You know, "THAT" person. The person you met recently. A friend you haven't spoken to in 7 years. That long lost relative. Whoever it was, they contacted you about an AMAZING business venture they'd just begun. They just needed 20 minutes of your time to tell you about it. We don't want to be "that" person. We want to build this business on kindness, love, and respect and NEVER be pushy or salesy!! We're trying to build a family, not a vulture-like sales force waiting to pounce on unsuspecting victims. Don't message people with a sales pitch and don't add them to groups or events without their permission. #facebooketiquette #dontcoldcall

---

Chapter 10: Generosity

One thing that is SO important to me is being generous. It's for sure one of my core values. As I said earlier, when I started this business in January 2014, our family was planting a church on a very tiny salary while I was working 3 jobs. When this business started growing, I KNEW that I had to give back; not only to God but to people as well. There are a variety of ways that you can be generous. So let's take a minute to talk through those things.

Time

Be generous with your time. Have you heard the saying – "time is money"? Your time is valuable, and so the giving of your time is kind of a huge deal. Spend time with your team and your members so they know you care about them. Please understand that this doesn't mean that you are ALWAYS available. You need time to yourself and for your family. I don't personally have set work hours, but Jake will shake his finger at me and make me put my phone down. #justkidding #kindof I don't really do well with balance, but finding balance in your TIME is super important.

Happy Mail

Be generous by sending happy mail. People always get super overwhelmed by sending their team and members happy mail because they think it needs to be this huge deal. #nope It doesn't. Send a handwritten note, a recipe card, or a sample of an oil they've been wanting to try. It doesn't have to be crazy. One thing that I've found that works well is knowing what is going on in their lives, and writing a note specific to that situation or event. This goes a long way in showing people you care about them as individuals and not just about what they are buying.

Knowledge

Be generous with your knowledge. We all know different things, whether from education, or straight up street cred. #imagangsta #okimjustmarriedtoone And guess what? We need both in this business. Share your knowledge with your team, members, and crossline friends. Being a team player is fulfilling, and it benefits you in the long run. Guys. My friend Rosy? She's a CROSSLINE FRIEND. Those relationships can be a great way to share knowledge! But be careful, I always tell people not to ask for something unless you're willing to give something back. Otherwise you're not a crossline collaborator.... you're a mooch. And no one likes a mooch. Ever. #truthbomb

Listening Ear

Be generous by lending a listening ear. Sometimes people just want to BE HEARD. That's it. They don't always want you to have the right answers or offer your best advice. So zip your lips and open your ears. You can't really hear someone when you're talking all the time. #preachingtothechoir

Money

Be generous with your money. Our family gives to our home church. We don't do it to be seen…we do it because God has so generously blessed us, how could we not give back? #itsaboutyourheart #itsHisanyway Find what matters most to you, and give wholeheartedly to that cause.

New Member Gifts

I always make sure I'm generous to those who have bought their kit through me. I make them up a mini resource pack full of ways they can use their new kit. It has things like roller bottles, recipe cards, and basic information to help them get started. #becreative Think about what you needed when you first got your kit and help them jump into the oily life!

Gifts for the First 3 Months

The first 3 months, following the purchase of a kit, are the most important, and it's not because you make the Fast Start Bonus (25% of their PV). It's because they are READY and WANTING to learn more. They just invested money into this amazing kit, now they want use it. They want to make things, diffuse stuff and just plain old have fun with their oils. So, I would suggest sending new kit owners a monthly gift for the first 3 months to show them what all they can do with the oils they received in their kit. Thieves Cleaner is a great item to highlight, as well as our Savvy Minerals make up line, the Seedlings baby line, and so much more! Give them a few samples to try out if you have a couple favorites. Again, be creative. It doesn't have to be fancy.

Rank Gifts

This is something that I'm trying to get better at personally. I was never given Rank Gifts until I hit higher ranks, but I feel like I would've been really excited to get something in the mail. Think about when you hit Star, Senior Star or even Executive. Those are HUGE milestones. Share the excitement with your team. Even if it's a nice card with 15 drops of an oil they may not have. Pick something up at Hobby Lobby for their office. It really doesn't matter, as long as it's tasteful. Most of the time people just love to feel appreciated and know that you're cheering them on.

Other Ideas for Giving

There are so many ways that we can be generous. Make it important in your business. Giving things away through social media has really helped me see that people are still watching and seeing my posts. It's amazing what generosity will do for your business.

I fully believe that God has blessed my business because my husband and I chose to be generous from the get-go. We love to give stuff away, to members and business builders alike! Here's why I'm sharing this; one of my business people let me know that she purchased her kit from me rather than another friend because she saw my generosity and wanted to be a part of that! WOW! Totally humbling. I had no idea how much our generosity inspired people until that moment. I'm challenging you to start thinking about what you can give away this month. This by no means is meant to be a guilt trip; it's meant to encourage you. I don't just believe in the blessing of generosity, I have seen it play out in my life. I want you to be able to experience the same thing. There's no better time than the present to start giving. It does not need to be anything big, just start the practice of being generous.

Then pray that God would bless your gift giving. People are watching you. Give them a great picture of generosity, and I know from experience, if nothing else, it will build trust.

#protip

Being generous means being vulnerable. It means putting yourself out there with the potential of getting hurt. And at times, you will be. There will absolutely be people who take advantage of your generosity. I get it. It sucks. But don't let the actions of a few spoil the benefit that your generosity will be to many. #theblessingsoutweighthepain

---

Chapter 11: Confessions of a Reluctant Whisperer

Remember my friend Rosy Crescitelli? Rosy is a crossline friend whom I consider family. She has an incredible story and a brilliant mind. She is a Certified Clinical Aromatherapist, is Healing Touch Level 1 certified and holds an Aroma Freedom Technique certification. Basically, essential oils are her jam, and she knows what she's talking about. But the process of Downline Whispering didn't come natural to her at first, even though she's also all heart.

Rosy is basically one of the sweetest people you will ever meet. I love her heart and her spirit. She is a big reason I'm writing this book. She is now a rockstar Downline Whisperer, and I love seeing how it has benefited her and her team. Although Downline Whispering is something that came completely natural to me, it isn't so natural for everyone at first. This is what Rosy has to say about Downline Whispering.

Rosy's Downline Whispering Journey

"Okay. I have a confession to make. I hate the Virtual Office. AH! THERE I SAID IT! I am a words girl. I LOVE to read, and love to talk. I DON'T DO

NUMBERS. They make me sweat. I get legit anxiety over numbers of any kind. When I told Beth that I NEVER checked my OGV and rarely logged into my Virtual Office, she pretty much had a fit. When she offered to teach me her wondrous ways, I have to admit that I was a reluctant learner. Do you want to know what made me a believer? Connection. I am 63% Yellow and 29% Blue. Translation: I love people...the more the better...I am an empath too and can feel all the feels all the time...I also love to have fun...numbers are not fun. LOL I am VERY little Green and Red, the colors that like organization, numbers, and logic. (Learn more about color personalities at jacobadamo.com.) I LOVE to love on people, especially the people God has blessed me with in my organization. After hearing Beth out and realizing how, by looking at the numbers, I can increase the connection I have with my people, I was all in. I use the information that I get from clicking through my downline or reports to reach out to people to let them know they are SEEN. They are LOVED. They are APPRECIATED. I send out private messages like "AH! Your downline is beautiful! You are really set up for success!" or I will notice that they consistently have new members over 100PV so I will ask "How do you do that? That is so awesome!!!". Then I will ask them to share with the rest of the team how they are killing it in their business. Downline Whispering has allowed me to really be intentional with my people. It has allowed me to find shining stars and give them a chance to shine their light to others.

Do you want to know what my favorite day of the month is? The very first day when all the numbers are at 0! LOL In all seriousness, the first is my favorite day because I go into my reports, choose the previous month, and click on "Rank Advancement." I take a whole day and write down the names and ranks of the people who made an advancement, and then I write them each a hand-written note. Since "Gifts" is my love language, I also have a box of gifts that I send to each person based on the rank that they have reached. Because of Downline Whispering, I KNOW who these people are. I have usually messaged or commented on the celebratory posts in our business group (if you don't do this...you SHOULD...it will change the culture in your group and truly make your people connect and love on one another). It is my favorite day of the month because I record all of the numbers (new members, ER %, total members, and number of new ranks)....but since I don't like numbers, I choose to see hard work, dedication, the changes that people are making in their lives, and the lives of their friends and family. It is a day of gratitude, celebration, and reflection. Sidebar: This "Rank Advancement" Report is awesome because you can also celebrate the people who were able to get to a rank that they reached previously. What a beautiful thing to celebrate someone who made it

BACK to a milestone! I love this new feature.

I will be forever grateful to Beth for having the patience to teach me how to combine my strengths as a connector of people with my weakness of number crunching to keep my fingertips on the pulse of my team.

Rosy Crescitelli
www.wholeheartedrosyblog.com

Just Stick With It

Rosy is not alone in this journey of being a reluctant Whisperer. Stay encouraged. There are many days where it's difficult or frustrating, and you want to quit. I get it. I pray that this chapter has given you a peek at why it's important to be a Downline Whisperer, even if it's not your first instinct. Being able to love on your members through this way of leading is beautiful, it will change your life and the lives of your members.

Chapter 12: The End is Just the Beginning

The end is just the beginning...if I'm honest, I always did think this saying was a little cheesy. But I'm going to be a little cheesy, because I'm kinda cheesy in real life anyway. When it comes to reading this book, it is nearing the end of our time together and now it's time for you to get to work. See what I did there? But I'm serious. You can read this book until you're blue in the face, take lots of notes and even tell all your friends ALL about it (which I would greatly appreciate #please #thankyou), but it won't do you a lick of good. Downline Whispering takes work. Work that will give you immense pride. The relationships you build during this business could perhaps be the kind that change you forever, if you'll just open yourself up. Be vulnerable. Work hard. Love harder.

As you finish, please understand that this doesn't even touch what your Virtual Office or Oily Tools can do for your business. There is so much value in running reports, delving deep into your downline and knowing your members.

The most important thing is for you to figure out a system that works for you. There are so many different personalities, and there is not a one size fits all for Downline Whispering. It may take you a little while to really be able to fully wrap your head around what works for you. #thatsokay Or you may have realized that you already do all of this, and you're a full-fledged Downline Whisperer and didn't even know it. #booyah

Always remember that Downline Whispering is about OTHERS and not YOU. When you focus on your team and your members, you're able to see the fruit of your labor in their success, whether they are using the products or sharing with their friends. #notaboutyou

Don't let all of this information overwhelm you, rather let it serve as a wakeup call. This is as good a time as any to start Downline Whispering. Will it transform your business? I totally believe that it will, and I am praying that it does - because I've seen it transform so many other people's businesses. You get to connect deeper and love harder. I'm not promising all fun and games, but I am promising a huge personal, emotional reward for you. If nothing else, you will find friendship and love. That is worth more than the money. I promise you.

I want to sincerely thank you for taking the time to read this book. I really hope and pray it's more than just a good read, I want it to impact you knowing and growing your team. Know that I'm praying for you and YOUR TEAM as you finish reading, because you and each one of your members matter.

Epilogue
"Doubter to Devoted" by Jake Whicker

When my wife asked me to write a chapter about my own journey in this business, I was hesitant; I didn't think it would fit with the overall flow of the book. However, after working with her closely on this venture, I realized it might actually prove to be very beneficial for you. Why? Because I have met scores of women who, like Beth, have had a similar obstacle; getting their spouse/significant other to "buy-in." This is an all too familiar refrain, and I would like to offer help. Now, I'm not going to mislead you and pretend I have some magic-bullet that will guarantee complete devotion from those you need it from most. What I will do, however, is give you some real world examples of how Beth turned me from someone who completely doubted everything about the oils and this company, to someone who is now totally devoted to the product and Team Young Living. I was a skeptic from the get go, so, Beth had quite the mountain to climb to win me over.

Beth has already told you about our previous endeavors in the Multi-Level Marketing world; how they didn't end well and ended up causing us to make a vow to never pursue anything like this again. We were both serious; she just wore down easier than I did. Like Beth, I have a stubborn streak. In fact, one of the things that our pastor noticed during our premarital counseling course was how similar these stubborn streaks were. It was of such concern that Beth even asked whether we should get married. Obviously, you can see from this example that I'm much more steadfast (she'd say stubborn) than her. After all, after taking Beyonce's advice, I wore her down enough to put a ring on it. Anyway, because of my stubborn streak, I will fight for what I believe in. At times, I've been known to continue to fight when I should have let it go. However, once I have been burned too many times, I will tear down the bridge and move on. This is exactly what happened with me and the other MLM's. I felt as if I had been badly burned; there was no way I was going to willingly expose myself to that same misery again. And boy was I determined. When Beth told me of her foray into Young Living Essential Oils, I said, "that's fine. But I DO NOT want my name associated with this business in any way, shape, or form." And so it began. This is how our journey into this business started.

As I said, I had been burned too many times to give this thing a chance. On top of that, there was no way that these "snake-oils" could actually help anything. But the real reason, in my mind, was the fact that I was a pastor. I had heard so many horror stories of people who went over to visit a pastor, thinking they were going over for relationship building, only to end up being presented with an MLM product or business opportunity. I wasn't going to have any part in such tom-foolery. That would not be me. I wanted people to know that I cared about them; that when we invited them over, we really wanted to get to know them, not sell them something. At this point, you had a perfect trifecta: I didn't believe in the product, I was leery of the business, and I was sure it would interfere with my ability to love and lead people as a pastor. So, I was out. I would not, nor would I ever, be a part of doing this business. The funny thing is, there's a reason they say, "never say never."

Over the course of the first couple months of her going full speed ahead, I can remember Beth and I having a couple of conversations regarding the business. She asked me one time what it would take for me to believe that this business was the real deal. I jokingly told her that if she earned $1000 in a given month, that she would convert me into a believer. In my mind I'm thinking, "ain't no way she's ever going to do that." I thought I was out of the woods. Little did I know how hard she was working, and how good she was at it. Hilariously, within the first three months, Beth comes to me with a check for, you guessed it, $1000. I couldn't believe it. On the inside I was speechless, but being the smart aleck that I am, I told her, "that's cool. Let's make it $1500." Within a couple more months, she had eclipsed this amount as well. At this point, Beth had definitely surprised me. I realized that she could make money doing this business. However, for me, it's never been about the money. Of course, money is important, and we should be as wise as possible to earn, invest, save, etc... But for Beth and me, the most important thing has always been the people. Since I still didn't believe in the oils and my concern about it negatively impacting my ability to lead people at the church hadn't been allayed, I was far from jumping on board. But my interest had been peaked. It's the things that Beth did next, that really changed my mind and made me jump all in.

Recently, while on a trip to my family's house in Central Florida, we went to one of the outlet malls in Orlando. As we were walking down one of the corridors, a man approached us and said, "I have a deal for you." Before he could get another word out, I said, "no thank you. We're good." It was as if I had said nothing at all. The man just kept right on. "For just $159 you can enjoy three days...". I kept walking and repeated what I had just said. Later that day, one of my daughters came up to me and said, "that guy at the outlet scared me." I'm sure many of us have been in a similar situation at some point in our lives. A sales person approaches us and tries their hardest to get us to purchase their product. They ignore our desire for them to stop and keep forging ahead in order to get the sale. I really despise this type of sales approach. I've worked sales as well, but I always made sure I was not "this" person. To be honest, this is how I viewed all MLM's; they were the guy at the outlet mall who steamrolled everyone in order to make the sale. Why would Young Living be any different? Yet, to my astonishment, what Beth was doing was MUCH different. What I saw was Beth, and the people with whom she was working, genuinely caring for people. The relationships seemed to be more important than the sale. This is what really began to soften my heart. But there were several different aspects of the relationship building that I noticed. These are the steps that Beth took to change me from a doubter to someone who was devoted.

When my college basketball coach asked the team if we knew how to spell with word "love", we looked at him incredulously. We were COLLEGE athletes. Of course, we knew how to spell love. "L.O.V.E." Boom! Nailed it. Then he looked at us and said, "you spell love - T. I. M. E." His point was that the only way you could truly grow to love someone, then effectively exhibit that love to them, was by spending quality time with that person. Without T.I.M.E. you couldn't have real relationships. Over the years I have grown to see the wisdom in that lesson. And it was love (T.I.M.E) that really began to chip away at the concrete that surrounded my heart.

What I saw in Beth's business, was people who actually cared enough for others, that they took the time to be with them. Granted, most of the time was spent via social media, but it was time, nonetheless. I could see authentic relationships being built. It was about more than just making money or making the sale; it was about creating a family atmosphere and taking care of each other. I was beginning to see chinks in the armor that was my resistance to the oils and the business. But I still wasn't on board. It would take more for me to be convinced. What convinced me was the way Beth spent her time.

You've got to understand something about me, I'm a pastor. So, naturally, I'm a sucker for the acrostic. You know, where one word spells out other words. In this instance, we're talking about the time Beth invested in her people. Well, time is more than just what's on a watch; it's about the details of that time. It's about **T**rust, **I**nviting **M**otivations and **E**ffectiveness.

What I observed, over the course of time, was Beth building trust with her people. And this was a multi-faceted approach. Beth started out building trust by exhibiting an extensive knowledge of and application for the oils. She worked long and hard studying the origins of the oils, what they could and could not do, and how they should be applied to assist others on their health journey. It became evident that she wanted others to experience that same things she had experienced by using the oils. But she knew everyone was different. This meant she had to know how different oils worked with different people. And that's exactly what she figured out. I could not believe the amount of time and effort she put into studying the science behind the oils and their uses. She really cared about people and the product that much.

The next thing that stuck out to me was how Beth was a salesperson, but she was not selling a product. She worked to sell herself first and foremost. She did this by making sure she was caring for the souls of people above and beyond making a sale. I would imagine that Beth has lost a good amount of money simply because she was more concerned about the person than she was about the profit. She has told people flat out, "Before you purchase this oil, let me give you a sample to make sure you like it and it works." This isn't to say she refuses someone who's ready to buy; she just goes out of her way to make sure no one feels pressured. This really had an impact on me. Remember, I have a strong dislike for those who approach sales like the "outlet mall guy." Beth was doing the complete opposite. She definitely wanted to take care of souls rather than taking care of the sales.

This is how Beth built trust. Here's the thing, she wasn't just building trust with those she was working with, she was building trust with me. I was beginning to see that you could work a network marketing business without the gimmicks and the trash. You could do it with character and integrity. This was foundational to where we are today. However, a foundation has to be built upon. And that's exactly what Beth did.

Have you ever been a part of something but you felt like an outsider the entire time? It's like going to a party, without an invitation, and everyone is standing there staring at you, wondering, "who let this guy in?" I imagined this being me in regards to the business; standing on the inside feeling like an outsider. Yet, this isn't what happened at all. That's because Beth, from day one, invited me along on the journey. How did she do this if I was explicit in my desire to not be associated with the business in any way? By playing me. Usually, when you hear this it has a negative connotation, but not in this case. What Beth did was she invited me along on the journey by playing to my strengths. What were my strengths? Well, I was a pastor, so I regularly dealt with difficult situations and the people in them. So, when she was having interpersonal problems, she would seek out my wisdom and advice. I now had a part in her business even though, at the time, I didn't completely realize it. Regardless, it didn't bother me because she was playing to my strengths.

But that wasn't all. Beth would regularly seek out my wisdom on where and how she should restructure her new business members. I really had no clue what I was doing when she asked, but I really enjoyed interacting with her and figuring out what the best plan of action would be. These were things I felt like I should be helping her with not just because they were some of my strengths, but because I was her husband and she was asking me for help. Again, she was inviting me along on the journey without me even realizing what she was doing. Now, let me say this. I do not believe, for one second, Beth had some master plan of tricking me into joining her business. I know she simply wanted her husband, her partner in crime, to be involved in the business in any way he could or would be. So, if you're wondering how to get your husband, wife, significant other involved, they need to be invited along on the journey according to their strengths.

One other thing that Beth invited me to do was to dream with her. As she mentioned earlier, I was the one that encouraged her to dream. I can remember asking her, "what do you dream about?" Her response shocked me, "nothing. I don't dream." I couldn't believe that. How does a person not dream? I'm a dreamer. Always thinking about the possibilities; of what could be. I could not imagine someone not doing that. After she told me, during the first year of our marriage, that she didn't dream, we started talking about what it meant to dream. At this point in life, Beth might be more of a dreamer than me. But one thing's for sure, she invited me to dream with her. The countless hours spent thinking about all of the possibilities this business could afford our family was key in my journey to fully supporting this adventure. You need to attempt to do the same thing with that person whom you need to be all-in. Ask them to dream with you about all of the possibilities that could be out there should this business be as successful as you believe it will be. I'm telling you, for most people, this will be crucial.

I feel as if motives are often overlooked in the business world, but the motives of a person, to me, are so important. Why do you do what you do? If I know you have pure motives in whatever endeavor you're pursuing, it's going to put me more at ease. That's simply because I know you care. In sales, it means I know you care about me, more than just the money. Money is important. As a prospective client, I want you to get paid and paid well for the work you did at selling your product to me. However, I don't want to feel as if I was bamboozled; like I was an easy mark just to make a few bucks. Now, there's no surefire way to protect against this; there are some great scam artists out there. But again, if you are upfront about your motives, I'll feel much more comfortable and confident about riding out this sale.

As I continued to observe Beth, I noticed that her motives were pure. Yes, she wanted to build a dynamic and growing organization. Yes, she wanted to earn a great living. But those weren't her only driving forces. She genuinely believed in the oils and wanted to help as many people as she could. She knew how the product had helped her, so she wanted to pass that along to as many people as possible. As I mentioned above, she was, and still is, constantly allowing people to try the product for themselves. And she's doing this at a cost to her business. That's generosity personified, and it shined brightly in her life. If your motives are less than pure, people will see that. Not just the people to whom you're selling, but those who are closest to you as well. Beth was beginning to wear me down. I was teetering on the brink of being all-in with her business. But I wasn't quite there. I needed a little more help

Help arrived in the form of Beth effectively communicating with me. This section you're going to read may start off a bit harsh; as in, "I can't believe the nerve of this guy." But my hope is that you'll bear with me as I lay everything out, and then bring it all back together. Just please try and withhold your conclusions until I've finished working through this. Deal? Deal. Thanks.

As Beth talked about earlier in the book, she never thought she would be in this position. She's just a simple girl who did not even have a college degree. Me, on the other hand, I'm the "deep one"; in fact, too deep at times. I hold a Bachelor's degree, several Master's degrees, numerous certifications, and I've even been thinking about pursuing my Doctorate. My fear is that you're going to read this and think I'm saying Beth is dumb, and I'm smart; please don't think that at all. What I'm trying to point out is that I was the one who had been trained to be an effective communicator. I knew the big words. I knew how to break things down. I would study for hours on end to make sure I knew what I was talking about in order to effectively communicate that with other people. Beth had not been trained on that level. She was a good communicator, but she wouldn't break down the nuances of a thing and put it all back together like I would. She wasn't worse than me or better than me, she was simply different. I will say that over the years, I have become a much better communicator by learning from her and how she perceives information. I would also say she has learned from me, as well. This is where we come back to that word effective. Beth effectively communicated with me in two distinct, yet crucial ways.

As I said, I'm a deep guy. I want to know that you have a firm handle on whatever it is that you're communicating before I'm going to trust what you have to say. That may seem harsh, but that's just the way I'm wired. So, when Beth would approach me about her business, I was absolutely blown away by the amount of knowledge she had about the product and the business. The way in which she could explain to me how the oils were produced, packaged, handled, and so on was eye opening. Then, when I saw her filming a video of the compensation plan, I think I actually drooled a little bit. Where's the Orange oil when you need it. Again, it has nothing to do with intelligence, it has everything to do with desire. Beth loved the oils and the company so much, she dove into learning everything she could. That enabled her to communicate with others and with me. What she communicated to me, above all else, was that this wasn't just some shot in the dark. This was a real business. She was an entrepreneur, and she was walking, talking, living like it. I was impressed. She was speaking my language. She knew the product inside and out, yet she could communicate it to me like I was five years old – because, in reality, most of the stuff she was saying would have gone right over my head if she hadn't dumbed it down.

The other way in which Beth effectively communicated with me is that the communication wasn't just a one-time event; she was constantly talking with me. Again, this showed me that she was committed to the business; it wasn't going to be like any other MLM we had tried. This was for real. Because she was committed and in love with the oils, it overflowed into her relationship with me. She couldn't stop talking about the oils, the business plan, or even the people she'd met. It was non-stop. In fact, she was on me constantly about how the oils could help me. Finally, I tried them. I don't know if I was desperate for something that worked or I tried them just to get her off my case. I guess in the end, it really doesn't matter. All that matters is I am now hooked on the oils because my wife consistently communicated with me the value they would have in my life. I am so hooked, in fact, that I carry around an Indiana Jones looking satchel that holds fourteen different oils. There ain't no shame in my game anymore.

Finally, after about 18 months, I was on board. In fact, Beth had hit Platinum before I was completely devoted to this business. But now it's full steam ahead. And it's funny how God works things out in his timing. About two months prior to this book being written, I resigned from my position as the Lead Pastor of a church in Columbia, SC. I was worn out and needed to recoup. So, through much prayer and counsel, we decided it was best to take a sabbatical. We don't know what's next as far as me and being a full-time pastor, but we do know what's right in front of us; Young Living. I've been able to travel with Beth all over the Midwest and East coast meeting, teaching, and encouraging many different people; people just like Beth and me. Who would have imagined that? I know I wouldn't have. Just a little over 18 months ago you wouldn't have caught me dead with an MLM business. Now I'm partnering with my wife in OUR adventure.

Hopefully, this has provided some hope and encouragement for you. I'm not naive enough to think that every single person can be won over. But I do believe that the things that won me over are the building blocks that will help you win over whoever it is you need to have all in. And understand this, there are different levels of support. Just because someone doesn't leave their job and travel all over with you, it doesn't mean they're not all in. Being all-in simply means that they're fully supportive of you and will sacrifice what they can to help you on your journey. That's love. That's commitment. Everyone's journey is different. Be patient and take the time to use the investment of your relationship wisely. I'm convinced that most people will eventually see the beautiful opportunity this business provides. Stay with it.

Jake

BETH WHICKER

Glossary of Terms

Active Member: An Active Member purchases products with a minimum of 50 PV within a 12-month period.

Commission Period: Young Living considers each commission period to run from 12:00 a.m., MT, the first day of a calendar month to 11:59 p.m., MT, the last day of a calendar month. The beginning of each month marks a new commission period. Only orders that are received within the commission period (or calendar month) will be considered for rank qualifications and compensation for the period's commission check. All bonuses, commissions, and rank qualifications are based on a calendar-month-to-calendar-month basis. Each commission period resets PV, OGV, and PGV, as well as leg status from the previous commission period. The required qualifications need to be achieved on a monthly basis for rank status. If the last day of the month falls on a weekend or holiday, the deadline will be the next business day.

Commission Eligibility: Distributors must place order(s) on their own account totaling 100 PV or more in a Commission Period to receive full payouts for their Sales Organization for that period. The exception to this is the Fast Start and Starter Kit bonuses, which require 50PV in orders.

Compensation Plan: How Young Living structures rank advancement, commissions, and bonuses for Distributors. https://www.youngliving.com/vo/#/resources/compensation-plan

Distributor: A Member of Young Living who purchases a Starter Kit and participates in the Young Living business opportunity as detailed in the company's Compensation Plan.

Distributors earn commissions and bonuses on sales in their downline organization according to their Rank.

Downline: Also known as a Sales Organization, this encompasses all members located beneath a particular distributor. This includes the distributor and all levels within his or her organization.

Enroller: The person responsible for personally introducing a new member to Young Living. Enrollers are eligible to qualify for financial bonuses, including the Fast Start and Starter Kit bonuses.

Essential Rewards (ER): Also called Autoship, Essential Rewards is a "loyalty program" awarding points to Members who maintain a monthly Autoship order of at least 50PV. Shipping date and contents of an ER order may be changed every month any time before the currently set shipping date. Benefits of ER include first-priority, discounted shipping, along with earning Reward Points that may be used toward free products, and loyalty gifts sent after 3, 6, 9 and 12 consecutive months on ER. ER members also receive a gift on the anniversary of their ER each year thereafter! Each point earned equals one dollar of free PV that the Member may later redeem for products, and while there is no limit to how many points may be earned each month, only 350 Essential Rewards point may be redeemed per month. Points roll over from month to month and expire on a rolling 12 month basis or if Autoship is discontinued. To cash in points toward free product, the member must place a Quick Order and select to use points on the payment page. Items with a blue flag in the VO may be purchased with accumulated points. New products are not eligible for purchase with points during the first six months after release. A member must still maintain their monthly ER order of 50PV or more in addition to cashing in points on a Quick Order.

Fast Start Bonus: This bonus has two parts: 1) You earn 25%

on your newly enrolled Members for their first three months' PV (with a maximum payout amount of $200 per enrollee per month), and 2) Should that new Member ever enroll a new Member themselves, you earn 10% of that new Member's PV for their first three months. NOTE: You must place a minimum order of 50PV on your account to qualify to receive Fast Start Bonuses.

Inactive Account: All distributors are required to purchase a cumulative of 50 PV within a consecutive 12 month period in order to avoid having their account dropped. There is no minimum PV requirement for a retail customer to remain active. However, if a retail customer does not place an order in 12 consecutive months, the customer's account will be dropped for inactivity.

Distributors who fail to accrue 50 PV in a calendar month are deemed inactive for that month and will not qualify to receive select payout from their sales organization (see Commission Eligibility). If an account remains inactive for a period of 12 consecutive months (the total cumulative PV purchased within that time is below the 50 PV minimum), the membership will be dropped from Young Living, and any agreements will be void (Essential Rewards Agreement, Distributor Agreement, etc.).

Distributors who allow their accounts to be dropped for inactivity will lose all rights to, claims on, and privileges from their previous Sales Organization. Upon losing distributor status due to consecutive inactivity, the Distributor's Sales Organization will "roll up" to the next qualified Distributor directly above the dropped Distributor. Reactivating distributors have no claim to any Sales Organization that was lost when they were dropped for inactivity.

Upon reactivating an account, all Retail Customers and Distributors must meet current Young Living enrollment requirements found in Young Living's Policies and Procedures.

Leg: A "leg" is formed by a Distributor who has 100PV and includes the OGV of his or her downline. To qualify for a higher rank, separate legs of the specified volume are required. Refer to Young Living's Compensation Plan for details.

Leg Requirements: A leg is the sales organization that extends below a particular Distributor. A Distributor must have at least 100 PV on their own account to qualify as a leg for their upline. If a distributor fails to qualify with 100 PV within a calendar month, the qualifying legs under him or her will "roll up," for rank qualification purposes, to the next qualifying upline with 100 PV. To determine which legs will be used for qualification, a distributor's legs will be compared against each other to determine which should be considered "qualifying" legs. After all, legs are excluded that might help a distributor reach his or her highest paid-as rank, any remaining volume may be counted as PGV, excluding any additional legs that are not paid at the rank of Silver or higher.

Level: The position of a distributor within a sales organization. Those distributors who are immediately sponsored by another distributor would be considered the sponsoring distributor's first level. Those distributors who are sponsored by a distributor's first level would be considered that distributor's second level and so on.

Link Builder: In your Virtual Office go to Member Resources and click on Link Builder, this allows you to have a free, dedicated link that takes your potential PSK buyers straight to the sign up page with your member number plugged in.

Member (Also Wholesale Member): A person who buys a Premium Starter Kit from Young Living Essential Oils and receives a 24% discount off the retail prices.

Month End: The cutoff is 11:59 p.m. Mountain Time on the last calendar day of the month. Month End is the cutoff date for processing online, phone, fax, and postal orders. To be included in commissions for a month, mailed-in orders must be received by the last business day of that month.

Organization Group Volume (OGV): The monthly volume of your entire organization, including PV, Retail Customers, and Distributors. OGV accumulates throughout each commission period (monthly)

Personal Group Volume for Silver and Higher Ranks (PGV): The monthly volume in an organization excluding any Silver or higher ranked volume and any volume included in the Distributor's qualifying legs.

Personal Volume (PV): The monthly volume of your personal orders, on your own account.

Premium Starter Kit (PSK): Kits that can be purchased to become a member of Young Living.

Rank: A Distributor's status within the Young Living Compensation Plan that determines qualification for commissions and bonuses. The 10 Ranks are Distributor, Star, Senior Star, Executive, Silver, Gold, Platinum, Diamond, Crown Diamond and Royal Crown Diamond. (See Compensation Plan)

Star: To qualify as Star in the compensation plan, a Distributor must achieve 100 PV and 500 OGV in a commission period.

Senior Star: To qualify as Senior Star in the compensation plan, a distributor must achieve 100 PV and 2,000 OGV in a commission period.

Executive: In order to qualify as an Executive, a distributor must achieve 100 PV and 4,000 OGV, which must include 2 separate legs with 1,000 OGV each in a commission period.

Silver: To qualify as Silver, a distributor must achieve 100 PV, 10,000 OGV, 1,000 PGV, and have 2 separate legs within their organization with 4,000 OGV each in a commission period.

Gold: To qualify as Gold, a distributor must achieve 100 PV, 35,000 OGV, 1,000 PGV, and 3 separate legs within that organization with 6,000 OGV each in a commission period.

Platinum: To qualify as Platinum, a distributor must achieve 100 PV, 100,000 OGV, 1,000 PGV, and 4 separate legs within that organization with 8,000 OGV each in a commission period.

Diamond: To qualify as Diamond, a distributor must achieve 100 PV, 250,000 OGV, 1,000 PGV, and 5 separate legs within that organization with 15,000 OGV each in a commission period.

Crown Diamond: To qualify as Crown Diamond, a distributor must achieve 100 PV, 750,000 OGV, 1,000 PGV, and 6 separate legs within that organization with 20,000 OGV each in a commission period.

Royal Crown Diamond: To qualify as Royal Crown Diamond, a distributor must achieve 100 PV, 1,500,000 OGV, 1,000 PGV, and 6 separate legs within that organization with 35,000 OGV each in a commission period.

Retail Customer: A member who chooses not to participate in the Young Living compensation plan, but purchases the product at retail price for personal use. Customers need to be sponsored and enrolled by a current Young Living Distributor and place an order at least once in 12 calendar months to remain active.

Retail Earnings: Amount earned by the Distributor from the purchases of personally sponsored Retail Customers. The approximate 24% difference between the retail and wholesale price of products. Distributor must have 100 PV monthly order.

Sponsor: The Distributor under whom a new Member is placed. A new member's direct upline. The sponsor may also be the enroller, but may not be if the new member has been strategically placed by the enroller.

Sponsor Placement Program: Members who enroll without selecting a sponsor or enroller will be added to Young Living's Placement Program. Through this program, the new member will be assigned a sponsor and an enroller with a rank of Silver or higher. If a member is placed through this program, the member or his/her assigned enroller may change the new member's sponsor within 20 days

Start Kit Enrollment Bonus: A bonus of $25 every time you enroll a new Member with a Premium Starter Kit. Example, if you enroll 4 new Members with a Premium Starter Kit, you earn $100. You must place a minimum of 50PV order on your account to receive this bonus.

Strategic Placement: Moving someone who enrolls with you under someone else to help build your organization. You stay Enroller (keep all the payout bonuses), and the person you move them under becomes the Sponsor. They get no bonuses, but the Sponsor will make uni-level commission on them.

Unilevel: Unilevel is a form of commission that is earned through the compensation plan. Qualifying distributors earn 8% on the sales volume, or PV, of each distributor on the first level within their organization, 5% on the second level, and 4% on the third through fifth levels. See Young Living's Compensation Plan for more details.

Upline: Any distributor above another in a sales organization.

Wholesale Price: The price paid for products by Distributors -- 24% below the retail price paid by Customers.